D1243598

Locke and the Scriblerians

Locke and the Scriblerians

*Identity and Consciousness in
Early Eighteenth-Century Britain*

Christopher Fox

UNIVERSITY OF CALIFORNIA PRESS
BERKELEY   LOS ANGELES   LONDON

University of California Press
Berkeley and Los Angeles, California

University of California Press, Ltd.
London, England

© 1988 by
The Regents of the University of California

Library of Congress Cataloging-in-Publication Data

Fox, Christopher, 1948–
    Locke and the Scriblerians : identity and consciousness in early
eighteenth-century Britain / Christopher Fox.
        p.   cm.
    Includes bibliographical references and index.
    ISBN 0-520-05859-3 (alk. paper)
    1. Identity (Psychology)—Great Britain—History—18th century.
2. Consciousness—History—18th century.   3. Locke, John,
1632–1704.   4. Memoirs of the extraordinary life, works, and
discoveries of Martin Scriblerus.   5. Scriblerus Club.   I. Title.
BF697.F68   1988
126'.0941—dc19   88-14201
                                                             CIP

Printed in the United States of America

1 2 3 4 5 6 7 8 9

To my favorite Munchkins,
Geoffrey, Sean, Annie,
and Ashley

Contents

Acknowledgments ix

Introduction 1

PART ONE   *The Altered Self*

1. Some Problems of Perspective 7

PART TWO   *Identity and Consciousness in Early Eighteenth-Century Britain*

2. Strange Suppositions: Locke's New Chapter of 1694 27

3. Of Porcupines, Problems, and More Problems: Discussion and Debate, 1696–1738 38

4. On a "Metaphysical Goe-Cart": Responses, Satiric and Otherwise 69

PART THREE   *Locke and the Scriblerians*

5. Of Controversy and Conviviality, and a Pedant's Progress 81

6. "A Master-piece" for "None but a Philosopher": Puzzles of Identity in *The Memoirs of Scriblerus* 96

Epilogue 119

Notes 131

Index 163

Acknowledgments

It has been said that the "past is a foreign country; they do things differently there." In my attempts to get around in the foreign country that is eighteenth-century Britain, I have incurred a growing number of debts. J. David Walker, Michael J. Conlon, and Vincent Freimarck sparked an interest; others have helped sustain it.

Among these, I should mention John Sitter, Patricia Meyer Spacks, and John W. Yolton, who read drafts of this study and offered valuable encouragement and advice. So did David P. Behan, John A. Dussinger, Jean H. Hagstrum, and Amélie Oskenberg Rorty. To them, my thanks.

At different stages of the work, I have had opportunities to try out ideas in lectures at Brown, Columbia, and Harvard universities; also at Cornell Medical College, at meetings of the Eighteenth Century Society, at the International Colloquium for the Historical Study of Locke, and in an NEH Summer Seminar in Philosophy. I thank these institutions and groups for providing a tub for various parts of my tale.

The National Endowment for the Humanities offered an opportunity to work overseas, with an independent study research stipend. I thank the Endowment for that opportunity, which helped this book. I also thank the staffs of the Bodleian Library, the British Library, the Cambridge University Library, the Edinburgh University Library, the Trinity College Library in Dublin, the Cornell University Library, the Columbia University Library, the Union Theological Library (and especially Seth Kasten, curator of the McAlpin Collection), and libraries at SUNY-Binghamton, Williams College, and Wilkes College. At the University of Notre Dame Theodore Hesburgh Library, Laura S. Fuderer has offered gracious and timely assistance. For other help, I thank Nathan O. Hatch, director of the Notre Dame Institute for Scholarship in the Liberal Arts, and my chairman, Joseph Buttigieg.

Paul William Child has helped with proofreading, and Cheryl Reed has shown patience, professionalism, and not a little humor in decoding the palimpsest I like to call copy. I thank her for typing the final version for press. I also express appreciation to Doris Kretschmer and Rose Vekony of the University of California Press, and to my copyeditor, Jane-Ellen Long, for their care with my work.

I also thank the editors and the American Society for Eighteenth-Century Studies for the right to reprint several portions that appeared, in earlier form, in *Eighteenth-Century Studies*.

It is a great pleasure to express my thanks to James G. Buickerood, for good talk and sober advice. To Patricia Buickerood, Michael V. DePorte, Frederick M. Keener, Donald Leslie, George Wolak, David and Catherine Schappert, Tom and Eilene Kaska, and my mother, Shirley, I owe more than can be recorded here.

I thank Judy for being there.

Introduction

my good friend, quoth I—as sure as I am I—and you are you—And
who are you? said he.——Don't puzzle me, said I.

Laurence Sterne

"There has been very great Reason on several Accounts,"
The Spectator tells us in 1714, "for the learned World to endeavour at settling what it was that might be said to compose,
personal Identity." Several years earlier, Shaftesbury states the
problem more succinctly: "That there is something un-
doubtedly which thinks, our very doubt itself and scrupulous
thought evinces. But in what subject that thought resides,
and how that subject is continued one and the same ... this is
not a matter so easily or hastily decided by those who are nice
self-examiners or searchers after truth and certainty." It is not
enough, Shaftesbury continues, "to use the seeming logic of a
famous modern, and say, 'We think, therefore we are.' ...
But the question is, 'What constitutes the We or I?' and
'whether the I of this instant be the same with that of any instant preceding or to come?'"[1] Shaftesbury was right. It is
one thing to say I exist, another to say I *persist* through time as
a continuous entity. This is the problem of personal identity
as the early eighteenth century understood it: more strictly
stated, the philosophical problem of what is meant by the expression "same person."

Shaftesbury's concern with this problem was by no means
private. The question he asks, and the question *The Spectator*
refers to, is one that pervades the age. In the same year as *The*

Spectator's comment, Pope, Swift, and Arbuthnot point in *The Memoirs of Scriblerus* to the "great noise" made "about this Individuality: how a man is conscious to himself that he is the same Individual he was twenty years ago."[2] Two decades later, in the 1730s, the Scriblerians' friend George Berkeley is still speaking of a need to "untie the knots and answer the objections...raised even about human personal identity"; and Joseph Butler attempts to confront the "strange perplexities [which] have been raised about the meaning of that identity or *sameness* of person, which is implied in the notion of our living now and hereafter, or in any two successive moments." A few years after that, Hume examines the problem only to suggest that the abiding self cannot be found and that the "identity, which we ascribe to the mind of man, is only a fictitious one."[3]

This study has two aims. The first is to examine what the Scriblerians call the "great noise" over "this Individuality" —that is, the extensive early eighteenth-century controversy over personal identity. The second is to show how this same controversy provides a meaningful context for the Scriblerians' own masterful satire of learning, *The Memoirs of Scriblerus*. For the Scriblerians take the language, themes, and often dry materials of the debate and put them to new and imaginative uses. They address, and in their own distinctive way attempt to answer, the question of "sameness" put by Shaftesbury. Finally, they echo a common concern—voiced above by Butler and Berkeley and fully confirmed in the statement by Hume—that something significant is happening to the traditional concept of the self.

In outlining an argument, I should also state some underlying assumptions. A glance at recent philosophical bibliographies will uncover a number of papers on the problem of personal identity and on the central figure in the early modern discussion, John Locke. Despite this interest, there is to date no full-length consideration in English of the discussion of identity in early eighteenth-century Britain. In addressing this need, my concern here is not so much in *the truth* about personal identity—a question I will leave to professional philosophers—but in historical truth; that is, in how eighteenth-century writers discussed the issue. John Yolton's *Locke and the Way of Ideas* (1956) traces the contemporary reception of Locke's *Essay Concerning Human Understanding* (1690), though not of his chapter on personal identity, added later. I hope that this study of the early eighteenth-century discussion of identity and consciousness—which turns out largely to be a study of the contemporary response to Locke—will interest historians and students of eighteenth-century philosophy and supplement Yolton's own.

In recent years, literary scholars have also addressed the question of self in works of the age. More needs to be done here, however, not simply in applying twentieth-century psychology to the study of eighteenth-century writers, but in looking at these writers (insofar as possible) within the context of the psychology available to them in their own time.[4] Since psychology in the eighteenth century appears in a wide range of contexts, a broad approach is needed, one that cuts across modern disciplinary boundaries. Exploring the early controversy over identity and consciousness and the Scriblerians' part in that controversy will, I believe, contribute to a larger understanding of eighteenth-century concepts of the self. Because of the Scriblerians' extensive reference to the world of early eighteenth-century controversy, *The Memoirs* were "even at the time of [their] first publication" in 1741, we learn, "fully understood only by exceptionally well-informed readers."[5] Despite a modern edition, in 1950, and three decades of subsequent scholarship, *The Memoirs* remain largely ignored. Approaching them within this early context will also shed light on a Scriblerian satire that deserves to be better known.

Part One

The Altered Self

1

Some Problems of Perspective

You *deny that we have any Consciousness at all, that we continue
the same individual Being at different times*. If so; it can be to
no great Purpose for us to dispute about any Thing; For,
before you receive my Reply, you may happen possibly to
be entirely changed into another Substance; and, the
next time you write, may deny that you have any
Consciousness at all, that you continue the same
individual Being who wrote this remarkable Sentence.
Samuel Clarke to Anthony Collins, November 1707

A good starting point would be to ask why the early eighteenth-century discussion of identity and consciousness has
not been better known. That personal identity was a concern
of eighteenth-century writers has not, of course, been denied
by literary scholars. Ever since Ian Watt pointed some years
ago to the age's difficulties in "defining the individual person," critical attention has increasingly focused on the issue
and its impact on literature.[1] And subsequent studies have
contributed significantly to our knowledge of the problem,
particularly in the later eighteenth century. But the same
studies have tended to ignore the emergence of the problem,
and the amount of concern over it, in the early part of the
century. They have also tended to downplay or even dismiss
the importance here of Shaftesbury's tutor, John Locke, the
first one in modern times to pose the question of identity-
of-person. And even when scholars have located this question
in Locke, they have often failed to see the revolutionary
nature of Locke's approach—something not missed in the
age of Pope.

There are a number of possible reasons for this neglect, some quite understandable. Chief among them is a tendency to see Locke himself as a noncontroversial and "safe" writer, whose doctrines were readily embraced by his contemporaries. Ignoring Locke's treatment of personal identity, scholars have tended instead to see the problem originating later, with Hume. Still another reason rests in our modern preoccupation with the self-in-consciousness, which tends to blind us to how strange this concept seemed when Locke introduced it. This same preoccupation also makes it difficult to perceive other ways of looking at the self, particularly the old theological vision of the self-as-substance, which Locke's theory had threatened and which his critics were determined to defend. Though there may be other reasons for the neglect of the early eighteenth-century discussion, these, I think, are the main ones.

The first rests in a prevalent historical misconception of the age's response to Locke himself. The rapid (and seemingly unimpeded) success of his new "way of ideas" tends to ease us into the belief that everything Locke said was immediately accepted. "On all questions of psychology," Ernst Cassirer assures us, "Locke's authority remained practically unchallenged throughout the first half of the eighteenth century." Donald Greene similarly speaks of the age "when Locke reigned virtually unchallenged," and Willey and Miller concur.[2]

True as such statements are about the extraordinary influence of Locke's work, they do obscure the important fact that many of his ideas were highly controversial. A necessary corrective balance is offered by the historical perspective of John Yolton and Kenneth Maclean. In the best existing survey of the relation of Locke to eighteenth-century literature, Maclean tells us that during the early decades of the century Locke's "philosophy was almost unanimously condemned in pulpit and pamphlet." In a study of the eighteenth-century response to Locke's *Essay* Yolton does not simply agree with this statement; he substantiates it. In a selective survey of the mass of pamphlets, sermons, and books Locke's work provoked, Yolton persuasively argues that Locke's "doctrines had a disturbing effect upon the traditional moral and religious beliefs" of his age and that he was indeed considered "one of the more dangerous...writers of the day."[3] One doctrine that disturbed Locke's contemporaries was his theory of personal identity, which first appeared in the second edition of the *Essay* in 1694. And our received notions of the philosopher's unchallenged authority should not obscure the fact that all the way from Edward Stillingfleet's *Doctrine of the Trinity* in 1696 to Joseph Butler's "Of Personal Identity" in 1736—and thereafter, in the work of Hume—Locke's theory was under almost continual attack in Pope's lifetime.

A second reason for the neglect of this early discussion may rest in the seemingly revolutionary nature of Hume's destruction of the abiding self in *A Treatise of Human Nature* (1739–1740). Even the best scholars, enchanted by the dazzling argument of the brilliant and suasive Scotsman, have often overlooked the earlier context. Leo Braudy, for example, in a fine essay on Richardson, dismisses the importance of Locke's theory and finds his context in Hume, who "does not demand the same fixity of personal identity." Yet it is precisely this "fixity of personal identity" that Locke's theory had threatened to the core. In her excellent *Imagining a Self*, Patricia Meyer Spacks likewise finds a context in Hume, certainly a valid one for the later writers she discusses. But when she suggests at one point that Thomas Reid and Joseph Butler "both write in the shadow of Hume," she may be overemphasizing Hume at the expense of Locke. Hume himself speaks about the "nature of *personal identity*, which has become so great a question in philosophy, especially of late years in *England*."[4]

When Hume says this, he is pointing to nearly fifty years of debate on the issue, a debate originated by Locke. In his own commonsensical manner, Reid is certainly responding in part to Hume. But Reid also penned a chapter titled "Of Mr. Locke's Account of our Personal Identity," tracing the "strange consequences" of that theory, among them this: "if personal identity," as Locke had argued, "consisted in consciousness, it would certainly follow, that *no man is the same person any two moments of his life.*"[5] Butler, writing three years before Hume, is explicitly reacting to "strange perplexities" about "the meaning of that identity or sameness of person" which Locke's theory had raised and to the implications drawn from that theory by Anthony Collins in an early debate with Samuel Clarke (1706–1708). Locke's "hasty observations," says Butler,

> have been carried to a strange length by others, whose notion, when traced and examined to the bottom, amounts, I think, to this: '*That personality is not a permanent, but a transient thing*: that it lives and dies, begins and ends continually: that no one can any more remain one and the same person two moments together, than two successive moments can be one and the same moment: that our substance is indeed continually changing; but whether this be so or not, is, it seems, nothing to the purpose; *since it is not substance, but consciousness alone, which constitutes personality*; which consciousness, being successive, cannot be the same in any two moments, nor consequently the personality constituted by it.'[6]

Butler's assessment of the conclusion Collins drew from Locke is, on the whole, quite accurate. This same debate over "personality" between Clarke and Collins also becomes the subject of an elaborate parody in *The Memoirs of Scriblerus*. More important now is Butler's—and, for that matter, Reid's—pinpointing of the source of the "strange perplexities" about personal identity, not in Hume and the later age, but in Locke.

Butler's comment also points to another reason why the early context has gone unnoticed: our modern preoccupation with "consciousness," which tends to obscure the revolutionary nature of Locke's theory and, at the same time, to blind us to other ways of looking at the self. That "personality is not a permanent, but a transient thing" and that it has a great deal to do with "consciousness" does not seem strange at all to us, the heirs of Proust and Woolf. But it seemed radical to Butler. Conversely, Butler's own position (implied above and asserted later) that personality is permanent and is made so by *substance* does seem strange and should remind us that people once felt differently about such things.

To understand Butler's negative response to the self-in-consciousness, it would help to examine some other contemporary texts. The first, published eight years before Butler's comment, has been variously attributed to Zachary Mayne or, more recently, Charles Mayne. In the introduction to this significant and neglected work, titled *An Essay on Consciousness*, the author tells us in 1728:

> There [is] no Account whatever of *Consciousness*, either now extant, or whereof even the Memory hath been preserved to us, by the bare mention of its Title, in the Catalogues of Books and Treatises reported to be lost; nor so much as any Notice taken of it, in the most elaborate Discourses concerning the Mind ... unless occasionally, or where the doing of it was in a manner unavoidable.

The writer goes on to assert that he is the first one ever to consider "consciousness" fully and "to put the candid Reader in Mind before-hand, that all the most favourable Allowances imaginable are to be made to a Work or Performance which is wholly new in its kind, or to the *very first Essay on a Subject*."[7] These statements in 1728 suggest, rightly, that the word *consciousness* and the concept behind it are "wholly new" at the time. Though the author's boast to be the first ever to analyze consciousness can be disputed, his claim as to the use of the word in his title appears to be nearly correct. In fact, outside of several minor uses of the word itself, the earliest written use of the term *consciousness* in the language is by John Locke. And in the sense of the "totality of the impressions, thoughts, and feelings, which make up a person's conscious being," Locke *is* the first. The *OED*, significantly, cites the earliest written occurrence of *consciousness* in this sense as book 2, chapter 27 of the *Essay concerning Human Understanding*. For it is in this chapter, "Of Identity and Diversity," that Locke sets forth his theory of personal identity and argues "that *self* is not determined by Identity...of Substance...but only by Identity of consciousness."[8]

Locke's use of the word in that context appears to be original. The received idea (passed down for decades by A. C. Fraser's popular and now dated edition of the *Essay*) holds that the word *consciousness* in Locke is a post-Cartesian import, borrowed from the French.[9] Yet, as late as 1808, in a translation of Dugald Stewart, Pierre Prévost states that "*Consciousness* is an English word for which I confess I have not found a particular equivalent in our language."[10] A century earlier, the first French translator of Locke's *Essay* had real difficulty with the term. In a long note to Locke's chapter on identity (2.27.9), Pierre Coste first cites Cicero's *conscientia* ("moral awareness," "knowledge of oneself") to suggest the connotations of *consciousness*. Coste then gives an elaborate explanation of the steps he has taken to translate Locke's term correctly, by "diverting" the French word *conscience* "from its ordinary sense, in order to give it one which has never been given it in our Language":

> The English word is *consciousness*....In French we do not have, in my opinion, any words but *sentiment* & *conviction* which answer, in any significant way, to this idea. But in many points of this Chapter they express very imperfectly the

thought of Mr. Locke, which makes personal identity absolutely dependent on the act of the man *quo sibi est conscius....* After having mused for some time on the means of remedying this inconvenience, I have never found a better way than availing myself of the term *Conscience* to explain this act. This is why I will take care to have this word printed in Italic, so that the reader will always remember to attach this idea [to the word]. And to make one better distinguish between this sense and that one ordinarily gives to the word, there occurred to me a device.... it is to write *conscience* in two words joined by a dash, in this manner, *con-science*. But, one will say, that is a strange license, of diverting a word from its ordinary sense, in order to give it one which has never been given it in our Language.... I confess that in a Work that was not like this... such a liberty would be inexcusable. But in a Philosophical Discourse one not only may, but must employ new words... when one has no aim but to explicate the *precise* thought of the author.[11]

Coste concludes by suggesting that, in French, Malebranche had come closest to Locke's meaning with a use of *conscience* in the *Recherche de la vérité* (1674–1678). Whether Locke and Malebranche were working from similar premises is debatable. Important here is that Malebranche never uses *conscience* in conjunction with personal identity. Nor do his earliest English translators, in rendering the work, change *conscience* into "consciousness."[12] Coste was highly regarded in the philosophical circles of his own country; his translation of Locke ran through numerous editions, was well received by Bayle and Leibniz (among others), and was used by the Abbé Du Bos to introduce the *Essay* to the French court.[13] If Coste were satisfied with *conscience* as an equivalent of "consciousness," why did he feel the need to alter the word? The very bulk of Coste's note, his laborious attempts to get at Locke's concept of "consciousness"—through Latin, through the various senses of *sentiment* and *conviction*, through hyphenation, through italicization—all strongly suggest that any easy identification of *conscience* with "consciousness" is a dubious one at best. The same factors also point to the originality of Locke.[14]

Coste's comments, along with those in *An Essay on Consciousness*, may help us understand Butler's adverse response to any suggestion that "consciousness alone" constitutes the "personality." Like so many early critics of Locke's theory, Butler is reacting to what is to him (though not to us) a thoroughly new and radical view of the self. That this same view does not seem strange to us accounts for a tendency to underestimate the importance of Locke's theory.

This same preoccupation with consciousness, which makes it easy to underestimate Locke, also makes it difficult to understand the position Butler and other contemporaries are attempting to defend. Butler's argument against the Lockean self-in-consciousness is that the personality is instead a "permanent" entity and is made so by "substance." On the face of it, this position probably seems as strange to us as Locke's did to Butler. What does Butler mean by saying that the self is "permanent"? Or by his use of that strange word *substance?* These are hard questions to answer, involving a context difficult for the modern scholar to reconstruct. But we need to examine the background here, because this age-old vision of the self-as-substance is crucial to our understanding of the problem and the Scriblerians' response.

Though the substantial self has a number of antecedents in the classical world, its medieval and Cartesian context is most important here. Amélie Rorty points out that the "idea of a person as a unified center of choice and action, the unit of legal and theological responsibility," is central to Christian belief. "If judgment summarizes a life, as it does in the Christian drama, then that life must have a unified location."[15] That location had been defined for the Middle Ages by

Boethius: *persona ... est naturae rationabilis indiuidua substantia*
("A person is the individual substance of a rational nature").
According to Étienne Gilson, this definition remained largely
intact during the formative years of Christian thought. As
late as 1710, in his *Tractatus ... de Persona. Or, A Treatise of the
Word Person*, John Clendon affirms that "This *Boethius* was
a Gentleman of Quality, had been Consul of *Rome*, and was
nevertheless so great a Philosopher and Divine, that his Definition of a Person hath been Authentick, and in Effect held
ever since."[16]

On this view, the individual is made up of both mind and
body, material and immaterial substance. The immaterial
substance or soul is by no means the whole person in this construct, but it *is* that indivisible and immortal part of him
which assures his personal continuity and ontological permanence. As John Smith asserts in 1660, *"no Substantial and
Indivisible thing ever perisheth."*[17] In *Nosce Teipsum* (1599), John
Davies attests to the survival of the substantial self, an entity
that will outlast "Time itself":

> As then the Soul a substance hath alone,
> Besides the Body in which she is confined;
> So hath she not a body of her own,
> But is a spirit, and immaterial mind.
> . . . .
> Heaven waxeth old, and all the spheres above
> Shall one day faint, and their swift motion stay:
> And Time itself in time shall cease to move:
> Only the Soul survives, and lives for aye.[18]

That this soul as "substance" will live "for aye" (and therefore insure one's personal continuity) is affirmed in 1678
by Ralph Cudworth, who assures us that the soul's *"Substantiality* is so Demonstrable; from whence it follows" that the
self will not "perish or vanish into Nothing."[19] As Gilson
puts it: "firmly based ... on the substantiality of the intellect

and the immortality it carries with it, the Christian individual" was thus "invested with all the dignity of a permanent being, indestructible, distinct from every other in his very permanence."[20]

If the substantial self provides us with metaphysical certainty of our own persistence as a "permanent being," it also assures us that we will be held accountable for our actions. Since all moral accountability (both in this world and in the next) depends upon a person's remaining the same, the substantial self thus serves an ethical function as well. As Samuel Clarke was later to remark, it "facilitates the Belief of...a future Retribution, by securing a Principle of *Personal Individuality*, upon which the Justice of all Reward or Punishment is entirely grounded."[21]

Descartes challenged the medieval establishment. But he did little to threaten the substantial vision of the self or its ontological and ethical assurances. In fact, as a well-known passage in the *Discourse on Method* indicates, Descartes supported the substantialist position:

> But immediately I noticed that while I was trying thus to think everything false, it was necessary that I, who was thinking this, was something. And observing that this truth '*I am thinking therefore I exist*' was so firm and sure that all the most extravagant suppositions of the sceptics were incapable of shaking it, I decided that I could accept it without scruple as the first principle of the philosophy I was seeking.
>
> Next I examined attentively what I was. I saw that while I could pretend that I had no body and that there was no world and no place for me to be in, I could not for all that pretend that I did not exist. I saw on the contrary that from the mere fact that I thought of doubting the truth of other things, it followed quite evidently and certainly that I existed; whereas if I had merely ceased thinking...I should have had no reason to believe that I existed. From this I knew I was a substance whose whole essence or nature is...to think.[22]

Descartes here moves from the question of his existence (the *cogito*) to the nature of that existence (the *substantia cogitans*). He begins by asserting that the self is "something" that thinks and therefore exists, and he ends by affirming, without question, that its nature is substantial. As *Meditations* 2 and 6 make clear, two points are important here to Descartes: first, when he thinks, he must exist; second, should he cease to think, he might cease to exist. From these two points follow the conclusions that he must *always* be thinking and that this alone presupposes an underlying, "indivisible" self or soul, "a substance whose whole essence or nature" is to think.[23] "By regarding a thinking event as inseparable from a spiritual substance," one historian of philosophy tells us, Descartes "assumed that it is dependent upon a persisting self." And from this "rationalistic standpoint," another concludes, "the problem of personal identity never really arose."[24] Thus, in not questioning the presence of the substantial self—of a "something" underlying and unifying the diversity of experience—Descartes carried on the old theological vision: a vision that assured the individual of his ontological permanence at the same time it secured his moral accountability.

With this context in mind, we can return to Butler's position and understand it more clearly. When Butler claims that the personality is "permanent" and is made so by "substance," he is defending the orthodox theological conception of the self. When Locke argues "that *self* is not determined by Identity...of Substance...but only by Identity of consciousness," he is shattering that old substantial vision. And what Locke offered in its place did not provide, in his critics' eyes, the same ontological and ethical assurance that the person persists as a permanent being. As they saw it, the new concept of "Identity of consciousness" led instead to an opposite conclusion: that the self is, in Butler's words, "not a permanent, but a transient thing."

Working out of an essay on Pirandello by Joseph Wood Krutch, Ernest Lee Tuveson arrived some years ago at a similar estimate of the import of Locke's theory. In his Pirandello study, Krutch had outlined a vision of the personality central to most classical and all Christian ethics, of "a fully conscious unity," a "soul captain," which "is an ultimate, even *the* ultimate continuous reality persisting through time": in short, the substantial self. Krutch then described what he considered a modern phenomenon whereby this "hard-core" character, "persisting through time," is replaced by a totally "fluid" entity, existing only from "moment to moment." Tuveson, however, locates the source of this shift not in modern times but two centuries earlier, in Locke. The dramatic ramification of Locke's theory, says Tuveson, is that no "unchanging soul is necessary to constitute the personality." As a result, "the personality itself" becomes "a shifting thing; it exists, not throughout a lifetime as an essence, but hardly from hour to hour."[25]

Tuveson remains one of the few moderns to see this as an implication of Locke's critique of the substantial self and his attempt to place personal identity in consciousness. But a point that still needs to be made—and a point clearly reflected above in Butler's statement—is the extent to which Locke's own contemporaries took this to be an implication. One of the central issues of the early debate is whether the self is something static, substantial, and knowable, or something fluid, shifting, and inscrutable; whether the personality is a permanent or a transient thing. To his early supporters, Locke had rid discussions of personality of an occult term, *immaterial substance*. To his early critics, Locke had severed substance from selfhood and had paved the way for the denial of the abiding self, a denial which appears to come earlier than Hume. Working out of Locke's theory, Anthony Collins told Samuel Clarke in 1708: "no Man has the same ... Consciousness to Day that he had Yesterday." Indeed, we "are not conscious, that we continue a Moment the same individual numerical Being." Clarke's response perhaps best suggests the orthodox reaction to the new view of the self-in-consciousness: "[Y]ou make *individual Personality* to be a mere *external imaginary Denomination*, and nothing at all in reality."[26]

As we explore the early discussion of identity and consciousness, we cannot then let our received ideas of Locke's unchallenged authority, or the seemingly revolutionary nature of Hume's theory, or our own modern bias in favor of the self-in-consciousness blind us to just how radical *this* notion was when Locke first proposed it.

We also cannot deny the Scriblerians' interest in such developments. The evidence points the other way. That Pope and other members of the Scriblerus group were widely informed of philosophical trends cannot be denied. Dugald Stewart praised Dr. John Arbuthnot in particular for his analysis of the philosophical "errors of his contemporaries." Similar praise was accorded Arbuthnot in his own time by George Berkeley, who dined with Swift at Arbuthnot's quarters in St. James Palace and afterwards described the doctor (whether justly or not) as "my first proselyte." In the same letter of 1713, Berkeley calls Arbuthnot "a great philosopher."[27] In a letter to Swift the following year, Arbuthnot suggests the truth of such praise, by turning his wit upon the author of *The Principles of Human Knowledge* himself: "Poor philosopher Berkeley; has now the idea of health, which was very hard to produce in him, for he had an idea of a strange feaver upon him so strong that it was very hard to destroy it by introducing a contrary one."[28]

Despite Swift's expressed contempt for matters theoretical, he, too, was conversant with current philosophical issues. As his *Remarks* on Tindal's *Rights of the Christian Church* suggest,

Swift also took an interest—and not a wholly uncritical one at that—in the current controversy over Locke's *Essay*. Since "our modern Improvement of Human Understanding," Swift says at one point, "instead of desiring a Philosopher to describe or define a Mouse-trap, or tell me what it is; I must gravely ask, what is contained in the Idea of a Mouse-trap?" Like a number of fellow clerics, Swift seems to have been suspicious of the religious ramifications of the "refined Way of Speaking…introduced by Mr. *Locke*," especially when this "new Way of putting Questions to a Man's Self" was applied by a Toland or a Tindal to orthodox Christian doctrine.[29]

Pope has been called the "first major English poet to write for a generation that had begun to think in terms of 'the way of ideas.'"[30] And of the members of the Scriblerus group, Pope appears to have been the most sympathetic to Locke. Pope owned a copy of the fourth edition of Locke's *Essay* (1700). Talks with Joseph Spence suggest that Pope had also studied it. In these conversations, Pope frequently commends Locke's style and especially the closeness of his reasoning, which Pope found superior to that of any of the French writers or even "any one of the ancients."[31] Despite his admiration of the philosopher, Pope too knew about the controversial import of the *Essay*. He was aware, for instance, of an earlier attempt to ban Locke's book at Oxford.[32]

That Pope and his friends also knew about Locke's theory of personal identity is evident in the Scriblerus papers. Kenneth Maclean says that an "interested antipathy for philosophy may well have been the corner-stone upon which Arbuthnot, Swift, and the young Pope founded the Scriblerus Club, whose records…abound in elaborate parodies of the fine points of the *Essay concerning Human Understanding*." Later, after locating one such parody (and there are others) of Locke's chapter "Of Identity and Diversity," Maclean adds that "one is greatly impressed with the knowledge of the

Essay that such thorough satire implies." Maclean is not the first to point to this parody. In 1751, William Warburton notes the Scriblerians' specific use of book 2, chapter 27, and elsewhere accuses Pope and his friends of some unfair "representation of what is said in the *Essay*"—a tendency, Warburton adds, which these "wanton wits" shared with more "serious writers" of the age.[33]

Not only do the Scriblerians parody Locke's theory, they also pick up much of the debate surrounding it. This includes a burlesque version of the most detailed discussion of identity and consciousness in early eighteenth-century Britain, the pamphlet war between Samuel Clarke and Anthony Collins. The Scriblerians' response to this and other Lockean controversies will be our topic in Part III.

Before exploring the Scriblerians' response, we will first look at the larger discussion. This is the function of Part II, which examines the discussion of identity and consciousness in early eighteenth-century Britain. We will first consider Locke's controversial theory, then central themes in the ensuing debate, conducted in the wide-ranging philosophical, literary, and theological circles of Pope's time.

That personal identity was considered a theological issue should not surprise us, especially when we recall that sameness of person insured eschatological accountability. But other factors also historically linked this concept with theological concerns. Boethius's influential definition of "person" appears in his *Treatise against Eutyches and Nestorius* (ca. 512), a defense of Christ's two natures and the related doctrines of the Resurrection and Incarnation. It is safe to say that prior to Locke, nearly all theoretical discussions of "person" tend to be concerned chiefly with theological doctrines rather than with the "personality" in any distinctively modern sense. For example, Augustine's central examination of "person" in the early books of *De Trinitate* considers the question only insofar as it helps us comprehend the Persons of the Godhead. (As a modern commentator points out, the "nature of the human person is relevant" to Augustine "only as an image or incomplete analogy of the divine trinity.")[34] In the *Summa*, Aquinas later places the issue within the context of the Resurrection and considers such questions as the possibility of this event in the case of a cannibal. How can the same man rise with the same body in this instance, asks Saint Thomas, when this man has consumed the flesh of other men? Such a culinary preference, he concludes, is only accidental, not essential. The substantial soul that informs the cannibal's body will remain after death and by a "conjunction to a soul numerically the same the man will be restored to matter numerically the same."[35] The doctrine, in this instance, is upheld.

The tendency to consider identity primarily within the context of theological doctrines persists up to the time of Locke's theory at the end of the seventeenth century, and well into the next. Robert Boyle, for example, in *Some Physico-Theological Considerations about the Possibility of the Resurrection* (1675) discusses the issue of corporeal identity at the Resurrection, given the rather grim fact of bodily decomposition. Though Boyle's investigation presents "one of the more extensive discussions of the concept of identity prior to Locke," the real issue here is the doctrine, not identity. The orthodox belief in the substantial self is assumed a priori, and whether the person remains the same, accountable agent is never under question, as it was soon to be with Locke. Boyle knows that "whatever duly organized portion of matter [the human soul] is united to, it therewith constitutes the same man" and thus "the import of the *resurrection* is fulfilled."[36]

Boyle's interest in the subject helps us understand why, historically, when Locke's theory appeared, it immediately became enmeshed in debates over the Trinity and the Resurrection. Or why the earliest references to his theory of personal identity occur in works like William Sherlock's *A Defence of Dr. Sherlock's Notion of a Trinity in Unity* (1694) and Matthew Tindal's *Reflexions ... touching the Doctrine of the Trinity* (1695). Another, more immediate reason is suggested by Yolton and shown in Swift's *Remarks* on Tindal's *Rights*: namely, that Locke's *Essay* was often appropriated by others and applied to orthodox articles of faith.[37] The concern with the traditional doctrines of the Trinity and the Resurrection—and the alleged threat to them by Locke's new theory—runs throughout the early eighteenth-century debate. The great controversy between Bishop Edward Stillingfleet and Locke himself, for example, was sparked by the bishop's attack on Locke in *A Discourse in Vindication of the Doctrine of the Trinity* (1696). Nearly thirty years later, Winch Holdsworth would preach *A Sermon ... in which the Cavils ... of Mr. Locke and others, against the Resurrection of the Same Body, are examin'd* (1720); and Henry Felton would follow with a popular Easter sermon at Oxford on *The Resurrection of the same Numerical Body ... in which Mr. Lock's Notions of Personality and Identity are confuted* (1725).

These critics of the religious impact of Locke's theory were not alone.[38] Locke was interested in the same concerns, and his chapter on personal identity is partly embedded in the traditional theological context I have sketched. The *Essay* itself, as Locke's *Epistle to the Reader* tells us, began as an attempt to arrive at a way of dealing with important *"Difficulties"* in *"Morality and Divinity, those parts of Knowledge, that Men are most concern'd to be clear in."* [39] It must have peeved the author of the *Essay* to be accused of confusing the very issues he had sought to clarify, among them the question of identity and the doctrine of the Resurrection.

We will occasionally look at this strand of the contemporary controversy. But my chief interest in exploring the early discussion is less in these doctrinal matters than in some questions Locke raised in new and exciting ways (among these, the startling possibility that the same man could, at different times, be different persons). Such questions have a direct bearing on the Scriblerians and broader implications for an age witnessing the rise of a new way of looking at the personality and the decline of an old one.

Part Two

Identity and
Consciousness in Early
Eighteenth-Century
Britain

2

Strange Suppositions
Locke's New Chapter of 1694

I am apt enough to think I have in treating of this Subject
made some Suppositions that will look strange to some
Readers, and possibly they are so in themselves. But yet I
think, they are such, as are pardonable in this ignorance we
are in of the Nature of that thinking thing, that is in us,
and which we look on as our *selves*.
John Locke

On January 20th, 1693, Locke wrote to William Molyneux
in Dublin, thanking him for criticisms of the first edition of the
Essay and requesting suggestions for the second.[1] The correspondence between the two had begun the previous year
when Molyneux, a co-founder of the Dublin Philosophical
Society and a close associate of Swift's tutor and lifelong
friend St. George Ashe, praised the *Essay* in a work titled
Dioptrica Nova (1692).[2] Because of a "Severe Cholick" that
had kept him bedridden for weeks, it took Molyneux time to
answer Locke's more recent request. When he finally did so,
on March 2nd, 1693, Molyneux reported that he could really
find very little to add to "the second Edition of your Essay,"
with the possible exception of two "New heads"—the first
considering the "Aeternae Veritates"; the second, the "Principium Individuationis." The former suggestion was never
taken up by Locke. The latter was. On March 28th, Locke
mentioned to Molyneux that though the actual writing had
not yet begun, "I shall...endeavour to satisfie your desire."
By August 23rd of the same year the work was complete, and

Locke told his Dublin correspondent: "You will herewith receive a new chapter Of Identity and Diversity, which, having writ only at your instance, 'tis fit you should see and judge of before it goes to the press."[3]

Such was the immediate occasion of the new chapter of 1694, which soon contributed to what Locke would call the "storm" raised "against my book." This was not the first time, however, he had mentioned personal identity. As Molyneux points out, Locke had already noted it briefly in the first edition of the *Essay* in 1690: "For if we take wholly away all Consciousness of our Actions and Sensations, especially of Pleasure and Pain, and the concernment that accompanies it, it will be hard to know wherein to place personal Identity" (2.1.11).[4] This earlier reference reminds us that, while Molyneux provided the occasion, the chapter owes something to questions Locke had wrestled with for years.[5] One such question, pertinent to "wherein to place personal Identity," shows up as early as Locke's *Journal* of 1682 and centers on his opposition to Descartes. Convinced as he was with Descartes that our existence is the first of all certainties, Locke was not convinced that thinking itself enables us to perceive, with certainty, a substantial self.[6] A second question pertains to ethical and eschatological accountability, a chief concern of what Locke called *"moral Man"* (3.11.16).

It was probably a problem with Descartes, as well as an interest in the issue's ethical importance, that led Locke in 1693 to accept Molyneux's advice. The next year, a man who described himself as "not, in my nature, a lover of novelty"— or of "controversy," for that matter—published what Isaac Watts and others considered a "strange and novel opinion" concerning the self.[7] He also sparked a controversy that raged in England for nearly fifty years, one in which he would soon be personally involved. With his chapter of 1694, Locke had managed, as well, to present what has justly been called the "earliest systematic treatment of the problem of personal identity in the history of modern philosophy."[8]

Though Locke held it the "more probable Opinion" that consciousness is "annexed to...one individual immaterial Substance," he had doubts about our ability to know that substance (2.27.25). The Cartesian conclusion, on Locke's empirical grounds, will not hold. First of all, that "the Soul always thinks" was not for Locke, as it had been for Descartes, a self-evident truth. "We know certainly by Experience," Locke comments, "that we sometimes think, and thence draw this infallible Consequence, That there is something in us, that has a Power to think: But whether that Substance perpetually thinks, or no, we can be no farther assured, than Experience informs us" (2.1.10). And Locke's own experience, especially his seeming lack of thought in sleep, informed him that this is not the case. There was no way that his discontinuous thinking could assure him, beyond a doubt, of a permanent and indivisible soul.[9]

Furthermore, as Locke viewed it, our knowledge of substance itself, both material and immaterial, is limited. That there is "something" underlying qualities he does not doubt. But he does doubt our ability to perceive that "something" clearly and distinctly.[10] After his investigation of our ideas of immaterial substance, Locke even goes so far as to deny our capacity to prove the immateriality of the soul. God gave matter life, Locke posits. Why, then, could He not also have given matter the power to think? It was this skepticism about our ability to know the soul that helped raise the problem of personal identity for Locke in the first place. "For if we don't know that the soul is indivisible, how do we know that it persists through time? And if it does not persist, in what sense can we talk about a person remaining the same?"[11]

If doubts about our knowledge of the soul led Locke to the

question, his concern for the issue's ethical importance suggested the need for an answer. To Locke, we could not simply assume a person remained the same, for in "this *personal Identity* is founded all the Right and Justice of Reward and Punishment" (2.27.18). Locke thus sets out to find a new way of insuring the persistence of the self against the possibilities of change, a new way of assuring ourselves that we are, in fact, the same accountable agents. In providing that new criterion, it also becomes important to sever personal identity from the unseen substantial soul, for, as Allison notes, "if personal identity were linked with substantial identity, we would, on Lockean grounds, have no clear means of determining the limits of moral responsibility."[12] It is therefore, paradoxically, a traditional concern for the ethical significance of personal identity that fostered Locke's nontraditional analysis.

Locke begins his chapter by noting that there are different kinds of identity. Identity itself, he posits, is an ambiguous term, depending on that to which it is applied. In a mass of matter, for example, were one part removed, it would obviously not be the "same" mass (2.27.3). In the case of living things, however, other criteria are needed. An oak, for instance, is the same oak not because of its material elements—which are continually changing—but because of its participation in the same life. When we come to human beings, identity becomes even more complicated. The question, Locke argues, cannot be restricted to substance (which will give us little assurance in the matter) but must be considered on different levels. In an assertion most orthodox contemporaries would find difficult to accept, Locke posits that human identity itself is an equivocal term. We can regard our identity, he tells us, in at least three ways, it "being one thing to be the same *Substance,* another the same *Man,* and a third the same *Person*" (2.27.7).

We have already touched upon Locke's treatment of immaterial substance, the first kind of identity. And throughout his chapter, he argues that the substantial soul is simply incapable of wholly accounting for human identity, not only because of our inability to know the soul, but also because this criterion leaves open the possibility of transmigration. "For if the *Identity* of Soul alone makes the same Man, and there be nothing in the Nature of Matter, why the same individual Spirit may not be united to different Bodies, it will be possible, that ... Men, living in distant Ages, and of different Tempers, may have been the same Man" (6). Locke also rejects the soul as *the* criterion of identity because of his belief in the absurdity of any claim that human existence can be considered apart from human body and shape.

This leads to a second kind of human identity, man. For "the *Idea* in our Minds, of which the Sound *Man* in our Mouths is the Sign, is nothing else but of an Animal of such a certain Form" (8). Locke illustrates this with the story of Prince Maurice's old parrot in Brazil, who "spoke, and asked, and answered common Questions like a reasonable Creature" (an example Locke discovered in Sir William Temple's *Memoirs of what passed in Christendom from 1672 to 1679* and one which Swift transcribed while preparing Temple's work for press).[13] Though this parrot could discourse rationally like a man and would thus fit the old definition of *animal rationale*, we would still not consider him a man, Locke argues, but a very intelligent parrot. So it is not the idea of a "rational Being alone, that makes the *Idea* of a *Man* in most Peoples sense; but of a Body so and so shaped joined to it." The material body and the immaterial soul must both go into our concept of human identity.

Thus stated, Locke so far has ostensibly upheld the orthodox theological view of the self, the union of the substantial soul and the substantial body. However, neither of these substances (taken singly or together) will on his grounds fully account for moral and theological responsibility. So he then posits a third kind of identity, person. Locke initially defines *person* as "a thinking intelligent Being, that has reason and reflection, and can consider it self as it self, the same thinking thing in different times and places" (2.27.9). This statement alone did not bother Locke's contemporaries. His next assertion did. The only criterion of *personal* identity, Locke continues, is not identity-of-substance but identity-of-consciousness:

> For since consciousness always accompanies thinking, and 'tis that, that makes every one to be, what he calls *self*; and thereby distinguishes himself from all other thinking things, in this alone consists *personal Identity*, *i.e.* the sameness of a rational Being: And as far as this consciousness can be extended backwards to any past Action or Thought, so far reaches the Identity of that *Person*; it is the same *self* now it was then; and 'tis by the same *self* with this present one that now reflects on it, that that Action was done.
>
> (2.27.9)

"Consciousness," in Locke's redefinition, here replaces the substantial self as *the* test of personal identity. How did Locke define "consciousness"? This has proven a hard question, in his age and our own. (Coste, we recall, had trouble translating the word in a way that did justice to Locke's extended use; and recent scholarly debates suggest that we are still far from a consensus on the question.)[14] On the simplest level, nonetheless, "consciousness" appears to be "the perception of what passes in a Man's own mind" and a reflex act that accompanies all other acts of thinking (2.1.19, 2.27.13). When, however, Locke applies the term to personal identity—which he was the first to do—the case becomes more complicated. In the above passage, "consciousness" might seem at first to be synonymous with "memory," or the present recall of past thoughts and actions. It has been interpreted this way by many modern readers, and eighteenth-century commentators on Locke, both supporters and critics alike, tended to do the same. In defending Locke against Butler in 1738, Vincent Perronet, for instance, tells us: "According to Mr. *Locke*, we may always be sure, that we are the *same Persons*, that is, the *same accountable* Agents, or Beings *now*, *which we were as far back as our Remembrance reaches*: Or as far as a perfectly Just and Good God will cause it to *reach*."[15]

Limiting consciousness to memory is, however, a reduction of Locke's scheme. For memory in his theory is only *one* mode of consciousness; and it is consciousness, not one particular mode of consciousness, that provides his new basis for sameness of person. In his chapter, Locke also often speaks of the "concern" we have for self, concern being another, important dimension of consciousness. As David Behan shows, Locke draws a key distinction between merely "remembering" an act and morally "appropriating" that act as one's own.[16] A moral person does not just remember his acts, he also "sympathizes and is concerned for them" (11). So "*Self* is that conscious thinking thing, (whatever Substance, made up of…it matters not) which is sensible, or conscious of Pleasure and Pain, capable of Happiness or Misery, and is concern'd for it *self*, as far as that consciousness extends" (17). It is not simply consciousness, but consciousness accompanied by concern, which helps establish moral accountability. This concerned consciousness, moreover, not only extends to past thoughts and actions but to present and future ones as well. "For it is by the consciousness it has of its present Thoughts and Actions, that [the same self] … is *self* to it *self* now, and so will be the same *self* as far as the same consciousness can extend to Actions past or *to come*" (10, my italics). In Locke's view, the "same consciousness" appears to serve as a unifying force that bonds together diverse thoughts and actions—past, present, and future—that constitute the same, accountable person.

Locating sameness of self not in substance but in consciousness would prove controversial. And at this point in his argument, Locke senses the strangeness of his attempt to sever substantial from personal identity. For he immediately turns to drive the distinction home. But it might be "farther enquir'd," he asks, "whether it be the same Identical Substance." He concludes that this question "concerns not *personal Identity* at all. The Question being what makes the same *Person*, and not whether it be the same Identical Substance, which always thinks in the same *Person*.... For it being the same consciousness that makes a Man be himself to himself, *personal Identity* depends on that only, whether it be annexed ,only to one individual Substance, or can be continued in a succession of several Substances" (10).

Thus, in Locke's theory of human identity, I can consider myself three ways: I am an immaterial substance, I am a man, and I am a person. Now, we usually tend to regard all three as constituting the same thing. But as Locke's series of puzzle cases show, this is not necessarily the case. Could one still be the same person if one's soul proved to be divisible, that is, if one's substance changed? Can two persons be attached to the same soul? Can the same man be different persons? These are puzzles Locke attempts to solve with his new criterion, identity-of-consciousness.

Could personal identity remain through a change of substance? Locke's answer, of course, is yes. For the main thrust of his argument is to provide a criterion of identity independent of any substance. To the question "Whether if the same thinking Substance... be changed, it can be the same Person," he replies that "consciousness being preserv'd, whether in the same or different Substances, the personal Identity is preserv'd" (13). Locke repeatedly, almost obsessively, returns to this distinction:

> For as to this point of being the same *self*, it matters not
> whether this present *self* be made up of the same or other

Substances.... This may shew us wherein *personal Identity* consists, not in the Identity of Substance, but, as I have said, in the Identity of *consciousness.... self* is not determined by Identity ... of Substance, which it cannot be sure of, but only by Identity of consciousness.

(16, 19, 23)

Locke's critique of substance becomes a major issue in the ensuing debate. By replacing "Identity...of Substance" (which we "cannot be sure of") with "Identity of consciousness," Locke thought he had preserved an abiding self. Others would see it differently.

Can two persons share the same soul? Locke here addresses the questions of preexistence and transmigration. "I once met with one," he puzzles, "who was perswaded his had been the Soul of *Socrates* (how reasonably I will not dispute. This I know, that in the Post he fill'd, which was no inconsiderable one, he passed for a very rational Man)...." Locke then applies his own criterion to solve this puzzle and determine whether the expression "same person" here applies.[17] Let any one conclude that he has "the same Soul" as "*Nestor* or *Thersites*, at the Siege of *Troy*.... But he, now having no consciousness of any of the Actions either of *Nestor* or *Thersites*, does, or can he, conceive himself the same Person with either of them? Can he be concerned in either of their Actions? Attribute them to himself, or think them his own?" (14). The answer, of course, on Locke's grounds, is no. Yet, should this same man have a concerned consciousness of Nestor's actions, he would find himself to be the same person as Nestor.

Can the same man be different persons? This question engaged Locke, and his answer surprised contemporaries. "I know," he states, "that in the ordinary way of speaking, the same Person, and the same Man, stand for one and the same thing" (15). But the terms *man* and *person* are not always interchangeable. Should, say, one's consciousness be either lost or transferred, it would be possible, Locke argues, for the same man to be a *different* person. The latter case, the transfer of consciousness, is largely hypothetical. Locke illustrates it with a puzzle case later picked up in *The Spectator*, no. 578. Should "the Soul of a Prince," Locke posits, "carrying with it the consciousness of the Prince's past Life, enter and inform the Body of a Cobler as soon as deserted by his own Soul, every one sees, he would be the same Person with the Prince, accountable only for the Prince's Actions: But who would say it was the same Man?" (15). Here, we obviously have a case in which the same "man"—the cobbler—is by no means the same person.

The other part of this puzzle, involving the possible loss or alienation of consciousness, is more central to Locke because it impinges on the question of ethical and eschatological accountability. What if someone loses consciousness of his past life? Is he not still the same person and thus accountable, both now and at the "Great Day," for his past actions? In answering this question Locke anticipates some criticisms soon leveled at his own theory:

> But yet possibly it will still be objected, suppose I wholly lose the memory of some parts of my Life, beyond a possibility of retrieving them, so that perhaps I shall never be conscious of them again; yet am I not the same Person, that did those Actions, had those Thoughts, that I once was conscious of, though I have now forgot them? To which I answer, that we must here take notice what the Word *I* is applied to, which in this case is the Man only.

Indeed, Locke continues, if it is possible

> for the same Man to have distinct incommunicable consciousness at different times, it is past doubt the same Man would at different times make different Persons; which, we see, is the Sense of Mankind in the solemnest Declaration of their Opinions, Humane Laws not punishing the *Mad Man*

for the *Sober Man's* Actions, nor the *Sober Man* for what the *Mad Man* did, thereby making them two Persons; which is somewhat explained by our way of speaking in *English*, when we say such an one *is not himself*, or is *besides himself*; in which Phrases it is insinuated ... the *self* same Person was no longer in that Man.

(20)

With Locke's theory, it is therefore possible—even probable, given the frequency of senility and amnesia—for the same man to be different persons at different times. It would then be unfair to punish Socrates waking for what Socrates sleeping thought or did. If they do not partake of the same consciousness, they are not, on Locke's grounds, the same person. The redefinition here of moral responsibility vexed some contemporaries, not least for its bearing on the Day of Judgment. As Locke implies above and later asserts, we will not be judged on the condition of our souls, but on the basis of our consciousness alone. God's "Sentence," Locke concludes, "shall be justified by the consciousness all Persons shall have, that they *themselves* in what Bodies soever they appear, or what Substances soever that consciousness adheres to, are the *same*, that committed those Actions, and deserve that Punishment for them" (26).

Insuring such responsibility at the Resurrection seems to have been a primary aim of Locke's chapter. As one early supporter, Catherine Trotter, noted: "if Mr. *Locke's* Discourse of *Identity* and *Diversity*, was design'd to resolve the difficulties that may arise about the Resurrection, that can only shew his concern to secure that Essential point upon every Man's Principles."[18] Nonetheless, this stand and others would embroil his theory in a half-century of debate. Locke recognized that his "Suppositions" here might "look strange to some" (27). He was right in his assessment of the contemporary response. The new chapter would soon be attacked on numerous fronts.

3

Of Porcupines, Problems, and More Problems

Discussion and Debate, 1696–1738

> What I told you formerly of a storm coming against my
> book, proves no fiction.... Shall I not be quite slain, think
> you, amongst so many notable combatants, and the Lord
> knows how many more to come?
>
> *John Locke to William Molyneux*
>
> If men could destroy by a quill, as they say porcupines do,
> I should think your death not very far off.
>
> *William Molyneux to John Locke*

Locke put identity and consciousness on the intellectual map. For years after the appearance of Locke's chapter, authors wrote—as Pope might say—about it, and about it. Stillingfleet, Shaftesbury, Berkeley, Butler, Mandeville, Prior, Watts, Clarke and Collins, lesser-known figures such as Henry Lee, Richard Burthogge, Thomas Burnet, Catherine Trotter, Winch Holdsworth, Henry Felton, John Sergeant and Peter Browne, John Harris in the *Lexicon Technicum* and Ephraim Chambers in the *Cyclopaedia*, anonymous pamphleteers and writers in *The British Apollo* and *The Spectator*— all were involved, at one point or another, in the early discussion of identity and consciousness. David Hume would join that discussion in 1739, and Henry Home (Lord Kames), Abraham Tucker (under the pseudonym of Cuthbert Comment), Edmund Law, Joseph Priestley, and Thomas Reid would later continue it, almost exclusively along the lines laid down by Locke and early eighteenth-century commentators.[1]

In the early discussion, three problems emerge as central themes. The first is Locke's critique of the substantial self; the second, his criterion of consciousness; and the third, the puzzles of identity. These three issues and the larger question they reflect are important to the Scriblerians and to our understanding of a key change in the theoretical concept of the self. The larger question these issues reflect is whether the self is a permanent or a transient thing.

Because we are accustomed to viewing the self in terms of "consciousness," it is difficult to perceive how revolutionary that notion seemed when Locke first proposed it. Many of Locke's earliest commentators could not understand how he could find the "same consciousness" compatible with the occurrence of forgetfulness and sleep. Others could make nothing of his equivocal definition of human identity, especially the distinction between "man" and "person." Still others tended, in reading Locke's chapter, to reduce "consciousness" to memory. What initially strikes a modern reader of his earliest critics, however, is their honest sense of befuddlement over what Locke is saying about the self.

Thomas Burnet, for example, in *Remarks upon An Essay Concerning Humane Understanding* (1697) accuses Locke of being "nice and scholastick, about the Notions of... Personality and Individual Identity." Because Burnet believes "the same Soul" to be "the same Man" as well as "the same Person," he cannot comprehend Locke's distinction between these terms. Indeed, he cannot for the life of him "understand what that Discourse about the Identity or Non-Identity of the same Man" means.[2] In 1702, Henry Lee tells us that while most "judge, that one Person is the same with himself at different times, only from the same Individual Principle of all his Intellectual Operations, my Author judges 'tis only from *Conscious-*

ness." Reflecting on the ramifications of this position, Lee concludes: "we think it hard to set up new Doctrines, without supposing the whole Frame of the *natural* and *intellectual* world alter'd."[3] Locke had created a new doctrine of the self. This is an early refrain. "How comes *Person* to stand for *this* and nothing else?" Edward Stillingfleet asks Locke in 1698: "From whence comes *Self consciousness in different times and places* to make up this *Idea* of a Person? Whether it be true or false, I am not now to enquire, but how it comes into this *Idea* of a Person? Hath *the common use of our Language appropriated it to this Sense*? If not, this seems to be a meer Arbitrary Idea; and may as well be denied as affirmed." Later on in the same book-length pamphlet, the fifth in a series of attacks and replies between the aging bishop and Locke himself, Stillingfleet again appeals to the "common Acception" of the word "*Person*," which he defines as a "*compleat intelligent Substance.*"[4] Here are drawn two corresponding concerns of the early discussion of Locke's theory: the replacing of the older concept of the self as a "*compleat intelligent Substance*" with the new doctrine of the self-in-consciousness. And nearly all Locke's earliest commentators, upholding the substantialist position, endeavor, in Henry Lee's words, "to answer all the Arguments which this Author has framed, either against the *Identity* of *Persons* consisting in the being the same Spirit" or for "proving *Consciousness* the *sole* Reason of that *Identity.*"[5]

Locke's argument against personal identity residing in the "same Spirit" shocked his contemporaries. Though he had stated that consciousness is probably "annexed to...one individual immaterial Substance," his theory (as his critics viewed it) had left little room for such a belief. By severing personal identity from substantial identity, Locke, they argued, had left consciousness in no recognizable relation to that substance of which it was supposedly a mode. And even more dangerously, by questioning our ability to know that sub-stantial soul he had brought its very existence into question.

These are some of the charges made by Stillingfleet in his extended debate with Locke between 1696 and 1699. Histo-rian, antiquarian, philosopher, philologist, controversialist, friend of Sir Matthew Hale, frequent preacher before a packed House of Lords, and one among a few in his age to urge "a more generous level of education for the children of the poor," Edward Stillingfleet (1635–1699) was an intellec-tually imposing man.[6] At the time of his death he was said to have possessed the "choisest" library "perhaps of any private Person of his time"—the library that nourished his secretary, the great classical scholar and arch-foe of the Scriblerians, Richard Bentley. From his *Irenicum* (1659) on, Stillingfleet had been a formidable Anglican apologist, "an Old Souldier in Controversys," as Molyneux remarks, who had "hitherto had the Good Luck of Victory," until he met Locke. Stilling-fleet had become dean of St. Paul's in 1678 and bishop of Worcester in 1689. Upon Tillotson's death in 1694, the queen considered Stillingfleet the logical choice for the archbish-opric of Canterbury, a post he declined, reportedly because of age.[7]

Though Stillingfleet and Locke were poles apart on some central issues—the question of religious uniformity, for ex-ample—they both enjoyed the patronage of Lord Shaftes-bury and moved in Establishment circles. They also appear to have been on friendly terms before the dispute, and Locke's new way of ideas had not seemed to bother the bishop until he saw its application in Toland's *Christianity Not Mysterious* (1696).[8] It is during an attack on Toland's heretical treat-ment of person and substance that Stillingfleet turns to Locke in the *Discourse in Vindication of the Trinity* (1696) and exclaims: "therefore I do not wonder, that the Gentlemen of this new way of reasoning, have almost discarded *Substance* out of the reasonable part of the World." He proceeds to argue that on Locke's principles neither could we have "clear and distinct Apprehensions concerning *Nature* and *Person*, and the *grounds of Identity* and *Distinction*" nor could we even "prove *a Spiritual Substance* in us" from the faculty of thinking. Stillingfleet closes with his own definition of person as an "intelligent Substance, with a peculiar manner of Subsistence"—a reaffirmation of a permanent, substantial self.[9]

Because of his reputation and position, Stillingfleet proved an embarrassing opponent. Locke complained in 1697 that once the bishop attacked him the clergy became "marvellously excited" against the *Essay*, which was discovered by "these doctors to abound in errors...and the very grounds of scepticism."[10] In *A Letter to the Right Reverend Edward Ld Bishop of Worcester* (1697), Locke tries to defend himself against these charges and challenges anyone who has read the *Essay* "to think I have...*discarded Substance out of the reasonable part of the World*." What he has said regarding substance, Locke tells Stillingfleet, has been said about our *knowledge* of substance—"the obscure, indistinct, vague Idea of...*something*" —and not about the existence of substance itself. "It is laid to my Charge," he argues, that I take

> the *being of Substance* to be doubtful, or render'd it so by the imperfect and ill-grounded Idea I have given of it. To which I beg leave to say, That I ground not the *being* but the *Idea* of Substance, on our accustoming our selves to suppose some *Substratum*; for 'tis of the *Idea* alone I speak there, and not of the *being of Substance*. And having every where affirmed and built upon it, That a *Man* is a Substance, I cannot be supposed to question or doubt of the *being of Substance*.[11]

What Locke fails to acknowledge here, Stillingfleet counters, is that this new approach impinges on the old ontology. Questioning our ability to know the soul puts its being into doubt.

This is a point Stillingfleet drives home in his two subsequent pamphlets. The question, he tells Locke, is not whether you recognize the existence of the substantial self but whether we can arrive, on your principles, at any certainty about it. You *"agree,* that *the more probable Opinion is, that this Consciousness is annexed to ... one Individual Immaterial Substance.* It is very well that it is allowed to be the *more probable Opinion*; but it seems without any Certainty as to the Truth of it." In fact, "we have no Certainty upon your Grounds that *Self-consciousness* depends upon an individual immaterial Substance, and consequently that a Material Substance may, according to your Principles, have Self-consciousness in it; at least, that you are not certain of the contrary." If this were true, says the bishop, there could be "no *Personal Identity* at all" after death and the Resurrection would be an impossibility. After lodging this charge and others—among them, the incompatibility of Locke's theory with the doctrines of the Trinity and the Incarnation—Stillingfleet again asserts what he believes to be "the true Reason of Identity in Man," which rests not in consciousness but in the "vital Union" between the substantial soul and the body. "I think the Identity of Man," the bishop concludes, "depends neither upon ... his Body; nor upon the Soul consider'd by it self, but upon both these, as actually united and making one Person. Which to me seems so clear and intelligible, that I can imagine no Objection against it."[12]

Neither could Henry Lee. In *Anti-Scepticism: Or, Notes upon each Chapter of Mr. Lock's Essay Concerning Humane Understanding* (1702), Lee argues that Locke likes to say that "no Man is concern'd for the same Substance ... only that he be himself, that shall feel the pleasure; that's true indeed, but the Question is, how that appears possible to be had without the same Substance?" The answer, on Lee's grounds, is that it is simply impossible for a person to "be himself" without being the "same Substance." Thus, we hear Lee repeatedly affirm that "the Mind of Soul of *Man*, with all its natural Powers united to the same Body, however various that may be in the several Moments and Conditions of life, is that which denominates him the *same Man*, whether an *Embryo* or *Infant*, young or old, sick or healthy, good or bad, wise or unwise, sober or drunk, sleeping or waking, sedate or passionate; these Variations not creating any ... reason why he should be reputed a *different* or *not* the *same* Man."[13]

In arguing for the substantial self, Lee also offers one of the more interesting early critiques of the new criterion of consciousness. His argument is essentially this: there can be no consciousness without a subject, no activity without a self. "Consciousness," he posits, "is only the repeated [*sic*] and successive *Acts* of the Mind, by which it takes notice of its own former and successive Actions: but *Actions* can't *unite* themselves; it must be the *Agent* that must do that." Indeed, that which makes these distinct acts of consciousness "the Actions of one Being, must be something distinct from the *Actions* themselves." That distinct "something" which makes diverse mental acts "the Actions of one Being" is the substantial soul. "That Substance then, in which these Operations are united, is that we call our *Minds* or *Souls*; but *Consciousness* is no more that *Mind* or *Soul*, than any other Actions are: no more than Motion," Lee concludes, is "the *moving* Body."[14]

A similar argument appears in John Sergeant's *Solid Philosophy Asserted, Against the Fancies of the Ideists* (1697). Sergeant (1622–1707), a Catholic controversialist, remains to this day (as he was in his own) a shadowy figure. At various times in his long career, he eluded the authorities by dropping out of sight, by passing himself off as a physician, and by assuming a series of aliases that included Dodd, Holland, and (even) Smith. As shifting as his own public identity may have been, Sergeant showed no uncertainty—in his critique of Locke—

over whether we persist as permanent beings. Like other early critics of Locke's theory, Sergeant cannot see "sameness" as an equivocal term when applied to this "*Individuum,* which is our *Self.*" A man must be the same, Sergeant argues, before he can be "conscious that he is the same." The fact that one is conscious of one's sameness presupposes an underlying substance. For one "must have had Individuality or Personality from *other* Principles, *antecedently* to this knowledge call'd *Consciousness*; and consequently, he will...continue the same *Man,* or (which is equivalent) the same *Person*" as long as he has a substantial soul. All the "Extravagant Consequences" of Locke's supposition that "Consciousness individuates the Person," says Sergeant, "can need no farther Reflexion."[15]

The defense of the substantial self, found in Stillingfleet, Lee, and Sergeant, is developed later by such writers as Berkeley, Butler, Browne, Clarke, Watts, Felton, and Holdsworth. Though all these critics question the impact of Locke's theory on orthodox Anglican doctrine, George Berkeley seems the most sensitive to the explosive nature of the issue itself. In private notebook entries in 1707–1708, he cautions himself, "lest offense be given," to "Carefully" omit "Defining of Person, or making much mention of it." Elsewhere, echoing Stillingfleet's opening salvo, Berkeley notes: "I take not away from substances. I ought not to be accus'd of discarding Substance out of the reasonable World." We have most "assuredly an Idea of substance," he later tells himself, "twas absurd of Locke to think we had a name without a Meaning." This, he adds, "might prove Acceptable to the Stillingfleetians."[16]

Though he generally heeds his own advice to steer clear of the issue—the word *person* is never used in *The Principles of Human Knowledge* (1710)—Berkeley does mention the problem in his later works, *Three Dialogues Between Hylas and Philonous* (1713) and *Alciphron: Or, The Minute Philosopher*

(1732).[17] In each case, he argues against the criterion of consciousness and for the substantial self. In the *Third Dialogue*, for example, Berkeley's Hylas posits the possibility that Philonous himself is "only a system of floating ideas, without any substance to support them." Philonous counters by asserting that he must be "one individual principle" because it is "one and the same self" that unites diverse and distinct ideas. "I know," says Philonous, "that I my self am not my ideas, but somewhat else, a thinking active principle that perceives, knows, wills, and operates about ideas."[18] Several years later, after arguing (like Sergeant before him) that "consciousness of personal identity presupposes, and therefore cannot constitute, personal identity," Butler closes his "Of Personal Identity" (1736) with the assertion that this "person, or self" that unites the diverse acts of consciousness "must either be a substance, or the property of some substance."[19] It is this vision of the self-as-substance that Locke's theory had brought into question and that his earliest critics hastened to defend.

If, as Locke's critics argued, he had threatened the concept of the substantial self, what he offered in its place had not solved the problem but exacerbated it. (As Butler would comment, Locke's "solution" to the "strange perplexities" he had raised was "stranger than the difficulties themselves.")[20] With the new criterion of consciousness, Locke thought he had insured the persistence of the self against the possibilities of change. He also thought he had preserved "the Right and Justice of Reward and Punishment" (2.27.18), which is wholly contingent on the person remaining the same. Not so, his critics were to argue—on both counts. Far from insuring the presence of the abiding self, Locke had, they argued, destroyed it, by shifting the locus of the personality from the indivisible soul to the floating ideas of an ever-changing consciousness. And far from securing a principle of moral accountability, Locke had, in his critics' view, simply made it impossible to determine.

All these criticisms are later lodged against Locke by Thomas Reid in his *Essays on the Intellectual Powers of Man.* "Is it not strange," asks Reid,

> that the sameness or identity of person should consist in a thing which is continually changing, and is not any two minutes the same?
>
> Our consciousness, our memory, and every operation of the mind, are still flowing like the water of a river, or like time itself. The consciousness I have this moment, can no more be the same consciousness I had last moment, than this moment can be the last moment. Identity can only be affirmed of things which have a continued existence. Consciousness, and every kind of thought, is transient and momentary, and has no continued existence; and therefore, if personal identity consisted in consciousness, it would certainly follow, that no man is the same person any two moments of his life; and as the right and justice of reward and punishment is founded on personal identity, no man could be responsible for his actions.

"I take this," Reid states, "to be an unavoidable consequence of Mr. Locke's doctrine concerning personal identity."[21] Early commentators also find this consequence in that theory. John Sergeant, for example, claims in 1697 that Locke's position "follow'd home, would, perhaps, make the Individuality of Man...alter every Moment."[22] Five years later, Henry Lee develops the same charge in attempting "to prove that *Consciousness* alone" does "not constitute *personal Identity*; and subjoin the *ill consequences* ... of placing it in Consciousness only." One such consequence is this: by placing personal identity in a changeable medium, Locke had made the personality itself a changeable thing. On Locke's scheme, Lee argues, we might "as wisely bury our Friends when fast *asleep*, as when they are *dead*. For when they are fast *asleep* ... they are not *conscious* of their waking Thoughts, they are not the *same* Persons." Furthermore, there would be no way, on Locke's grounds, of determining moral accountability, in this world or the next. For, if *"Consciousness* only" makes a person "the *same*," notes Lee,

> and the want of it a *different* Person, then no Courts of *Humane* Judicature can be justly establish'd. For how can any Judge or Jury be certain, that a man (during the Commission of any Fact, or entring into any Covenants) was sleepy or broad awake, sober or mad, sedate or passionate ... sober or drunk, tenacious or forgetful? For any of these two Circumstances may so alter the State of the Case, as to denominate him a *different* person; if the want of *Consciousness* can make him so.[23]

Along with Stillingfleet and Sergeant, Lee also voices another fear. By locating personal identity in consciousness and making both distinct from spiritual substance, Locke had opened the door to a materialistic interpretation of the self.[24] This charge also comes up in the 1706–1708 debate between Samuel Clarke and Anthony Collins—a controversy that would later be rewritten in *The Memoirs of Scriblerus*.

This controversy pitted Clarke, the Boyle Lecturer, chief lieutenant of Newton, and an individual considered by many the finest mind of his age, against a little-known friend of Locke's who was yet to achieve the notoriety the later *Discourse on Free-Thinking* would bring. (A reviewer of that work in 1713 would say of Collins, "if ever Man deserved to be denied the common Benefits of Air and Water, it is the Author of *a Discourse of Free-Thinking*.")[25] In its choice of topics the Clarke-Collins controversy is wide-ranging, and in its treatment of them, comprehensive, to say the least. A wearied Clarke would comment at the opening of his last pamphlet, the ninth in the long debate: "Of repeating the same Things over and over again, there is no End."[26] Whether the soul is immaterial and whether matter can think: these are the main questions raised in the opening stages of the dispute. Only gradually does it evolve into a heated discussion, in the later pamphlets, of the problem of personal identity.

Pertinent to our purposes in the early pamphlets is the discussion of consciousness, couched within a host of related topics. Throughout his first two pamphlets—first against Henry Dodwell, who initiated the debate, and then against Collins, who stepped in under the guise of defending Dodwell's contention that the soul is naturally mortal—Clarke argues that the immateriality of the soul can be demonstrated "from the single consideration" of "Consciousness it self."[27] The soul, Clarke says, is immaterial and will "continue its own Duration for ever" because it has "one Individual Consciousness," or the undivided quality of continuous thought. Matter, on the other hand, cannot be conscious because it is divisible into parts (pp. 730–31).

We have seen a similar argument before, in Descartes, and a counterargument, in Locke. Simply put, Clarke argues that consciousness is an undivided activity, that the soul always thinks. Thus, when challenged by Collins in a *Reply to Mr. Clarke's Defence* that "we know by Experience, that the Soul or Thinking Being undergoes several Changes or Alterations"; that it has "Powers" which plainly "cease for a time"; and that consciousness therefore, like matter, is divisible into parts, Clarke responds:

> It is true, my affirming Consciousness to be an individual Power, is not giving an Account of what Consciousness is; neither was it intended to be so. Every Man feels and knows by Experience what Consciousness is, better than any Man can explain it.... And it is not at all necessary to define more particularly what *it is*; but abundantly sufficient that we know and agree what it *is not*, viz. that it is not a Multitude of distinct and separate Consciousnesses.
>
> (pp. 772–73, 790)

The question of whether thought itself is an indivisible "individual Power" or whether it is instead "a Multitude of distinct and separate Consciousnesses" leads, in that latter part of the debate, to the most complete discussion of identity and consciousness in the early part of the century. In this discussion, Collins supports Locke and argues that "it is evident, that *Self* or Personal Identity consist solely in Consciousness; since when I distinguish my *Self* from others, and when I attribute any past Actions to my *Self*, it is only by extending my Consciousness to them" (p. 875). But Collins goes beyond Locke in pushing his theory to a conclusion Locke himself never reached. Against Collins's interpretation of Locke, Clarke defends the substantial self.

In *Reflections on Mr. Clarke's Second Defence*—the sixth exchange in the debate—Collins returns to his earlier argument that thought itself, far from being indivisible, is discontinuous, divided, and interrupted. "Thinking or Human Consciousness," says Collins, "begins, continues and ends, or has Generation, Succession and Corruption, like all other Modes of Matter; as like them it is divided." Moreover, if the "Soul or Principle of Thinking" is undivided, Collins asks, "how can it be capable, partly or wholly, to forget any thing?" Such dysfunctions are not explained, Collins contends, "by any thing indivisible" (p. 807). Indeed, he asks (p. 809), what "can better Account for our total Forgetfulness of some things, our partial Forgetfulness of others, than to suppose the Substance of the Brain in a constant Flux?"

If these points are valid, Clarke responds, personal identity would be an impossibility. It "is a manifest Contradiction," he says in his *Third Defence*, "that the *Consciousness* of its being done by *me*, by *my own individual self* in particular, should continue in me after my whole Substance is changed" (p. 844). Against Collins's contention that thought itself is divisible and changing, Clarke asserts the abiding presence of the "same whole Substance":

> The same whole Substance hears every Sound, smells every Odour, tastes every Sapour [*sic*], and feels every thing that touches any Part of the Body. Every Imagination, every Volition, and every Thought is the Imagination, Will, and Thought, of that whole Thinking Substance, which I call *myself*. And if this one Substance (which we usually stile the *Soul* or *Mind*) has no Parts, that can *act* separately; it may as well be conceived to have none, that can *exist* separately; and so, to be absolutely *Indivisible*. (p. 843)

To argue otherwise—to suggest that a person could survive a change of substance and that consciousness itself is not a "fixt" and indivisible quality but a "fleeting" mode—is to destroy the very notion of the self. If you argue, Clarke tells Collins,

> that which we call *Consciousness*, is not a *fixt individual numerical Quality*... but a *fleeting transferrible Mode or Power*, like the Roundness or the Mode of Motion of Circles upon the Face of a running Stream: And that the *Person* may still be the same, by a continual Superaddition of the *like Consciousness*; notwithstanding the whole *Substance* be changed: Then I say, you make *individual Personality* to be a mere *external imaginary Denomination*, and nothing at all in reality: Just as a *Ship* is called the *same Ship*, after the whole Substance is changed by frequent Repairs; or a *River* is called the *same River*, though the Water of it be every Day new. The *Name* of the Ship, is the same; but the *Ship itself*, is not at all the same: And the continued *Name* of the River signifies Water running in the same Channel, but not at all the *same Water*. So if a Man at Forty Years of Age, has nothing of the same Substance in him... that he had at Twenty; he may be called the *same Person*, by a mere *external imaginary Denomination*.... But he cannot be *really and truly* the *same Person*. (p. 844)

On Collins's principles, Clarke continues, along with the destruction of personal identity would come the destruction of the moral accountability that depends upon a person remaining the same. For "such a Consciousness in a Man, whose Substance is wholly changed" cannot "make it Just and Equitable for such a Man to be punished for an Action done by another" (pp. 844–45).

Nor would it be just and equitable for him to be judged at the Resurrection, Clarke continues, in a line paralleling Stillingfleet's earlier attacks on Locke. If consciousness is nothing but a fleeting mode of matter that perishes at the dissolution of the body, then the restoring of that consciousness at the Resurrection will not "be a Raising again of the *same individual Person*" but the creation of a new person. "This inexplicable Confusion," Clarke concludes, "wherewith your Doctrine perplexes the Notion of *personal Identity*, upon which Identity the Justice of all Reward or Punishment manifestly depends; makes the *Resurrection*, in your way of arguing, to be inconceivable and impossible.... But if the Soul be, as we believe, a *permanent indivisible immaterial Substance*, then all these Difficulties vanish of themselves."[28]

In *An Answer to Mr. Clarke's Third Defence*, Collins considers Clarke's charges and then proceeds to validate them, by taking Locke's criterion to an extreme conclusion. Since Clarke's last accusation, says Collins, is "founded on the Question of Identity, it will not be amiss to state briefly my Opinion, before I consider his Exceptions." Collins here gives his own opinion on the subject—nearly all of it taken directly from Locke's chapter—before arriving at that identity "which we signify by the Word *Self*, and sometimes call *Personal Identity*." To understand what constitutes personal identity, says Collins,

let us consider to what Ideas we apply the Term *Self*. If a Man charges me with a Murder done by some body last Night, of which I am not conscious; I deny that I did the Action, and cannot possibly attribute it to my *Self*, because I am not conscious that I did it. Again, suppose me to be seized with a short Frenzy of an Hour, and during that time to kill a Man, and then to return to my *Self* without the least Consciousness of what I have done; I can no more attribute that Action to my *Self*, than I could the former, which I supposed done by another. The mad Man and the sober Man are really two as distinct Persons as any two Other Men in the World, and will be so considered in a Court of Judicature, where want of Consciousness can be proved.

Repeating Locke's definition almost verbatim, Collins argues that personal identity by no means resides in the same whole substance but "solely in Consciousness" (p. 875).

After arriving at this opinion of the question of identity, Collins turns to consider Clarke's "Exceptions." And it is here that Collins begins to carry Locke's theory to a conclusion he never put forward. Clarke had argued that if personal identity consisted in consciousness and if that consciousness was only a fleeting mode, the Resurrection of the same person would be impossible. "To which I answer," says Collins, "if *Personal Identity* consists in Consciousness, as before explained ... Consciousness can perish no more at the Dissolution of the Body, than it does every Moment we cease to think, or be conscious" (p. 876). Though Collins proceeds to argue that "Memory or Consciousness extending to past Actions" will affirm personal identity, the direction of the first statement seems to be this: the personality is a transient thing. Consciousness, he again asserts, is by no means indivisible but "a Number of particular Acts" which "perish the Moment they begin" (p. 876)—in Clarke's words, a "Multitude of distinct and separate Consciousnesses." In fact,

no Man has the same numerical Consciousness to Day that he had Yesterday: the Consciousness he has to Day, is a dis-

tinct numerical Act from all past Consciousnesses; and can
be no more the same numerical individual Consciousness
with any of those past Consciousnesses, than the Motion of
a System of Matter to Day, can be the numerical individual Motion it had Yesterday.

Given the fleeting nature of these distinct and successive
acts, Collins argues, "we are not conscious, that we continue a Moment the same individual numerical Being"
(p. 870).

If this conclusion is not clear to Clarke, Collins advises him
to consult both Mr. Locke and experience. Both, Collins concludes, argue convincingly against the continuity of the same
"individual numerical Being," against the persistence of a
substantial self:

> When he…will give himself the trouble to consider Mr.
> *Locke's* Chapter of *Identity* and *Diversity*, he will see, that let
> him frame what imaginary Schemes of *personal Identity* he
> pleases, if there lie not unanswerable Objections against them
> all, except that of *personal Identity consisting in Consciousness*, yet
> at least that Experience perfectly contradicts his Notion of
> *personal Identity*, which consists in *an individual numerical Being,
> with the same numerical Consciousness.*
>
> (p. 878)

In responding to Collins, a shocked Clarke repeats several
earlier charges and adds some new ones, in arguing the absurdity of "*whether individual Personality can be preserved by a continual transferring of Consciousness from one Parcel of Matter to another, in so flux a Substance as the Brain.*" Clarke tells Collins that
he has evaded none of the earlier accusations: that he has
made "*Individual Personality to be a mere external imaginary Denomination*"; that he has made it feasible "that *One Man may
possibly be two Persons*"; and that he has destroyed moral responsibility (p. 902). Of Collins's demonstration of his belief

that personal identity consists "solely in Consciousness,"
Clarke remarks:

> *A Man*, you say, who, during *a short Frenzy, kills* another, *and
> then returns to himself, without the least Consciousness of what he has
> done; cannot attribute that Action to himself*; and therefore *the mad
> Man and the sober Man are really two as distinct Persons as any two
> other Men in the World....* Extraordinary Reasoning indeed!
> Because in a *figurative* Sense a Man, when he is mad, is said *not
> to be himself*; and in a *forensick* Sense, is looked upon as not an-
> swerable for his *own Actions*; therefore in the *natural and philo-
> sophical* Sense also, *his Actions* are not *his own Actions*, but *another
> Person's*; and the *same Man* is *really two distinct Persons*!
>
> (p. 902)

Besides such absurdities as this, Clarke continues, would be
the virtual impossibility of a *"true Memory"* in Collins's "flect-
ing Being." And so on Collins's principles we are all *"unavoid-
ably we know not who*, and do but *fancy and dream* ourselves to be
the Persons we think we are, and write and read about *we
know not Whom nor What."* In this last pamphlet of the debate,
Clarke concludes by asserting that Collins's vision of the self-
in-consciousness is destructive of all religion, because it makes
"a future State of Rewards and Punishments not only *Improbable*, but *Impossible*; seeing it infers ... an absolute *Impossibility*
of a *Resurrection of the same Person"* (pp. 903–4).

Though it is perhaps difficult for us to appreciate the fact,
the Clarke-Collins controversy was popular in Pope's age.
Nearly all nine pamphlets in the dispute ran through at least
two editions by 1712; and the debate was reprinted in its en-
tirety as late as 1731 and 1738.[29] It is also frequently mentioned in works that take up Locke's theory of personal identity and its implications, including *The Memoirs of Scriblerus*.
And it is Collins's use of Locke's criterion that Butler mentions directly, nearly thirty years later, in 1736. In a note to a
passage charging Locke's followers with making personality a

transient thing, Butler tells us to "See an *Answer to Dr. Clarke's Third Defence*." Though we have briefly noted Butler's charge earlier, it would help to look at it again and place it within the context of the controversy. For it picks up, in main, problems early critics saw in the new view of identity-in-consciousness. "Mr. Locke's observations upon this subject appear hasty," says Butler,

> and he seems to profess himself dissatisfied with suppositions, which he has made relating it. But some of those hasty observations have been carried to a strange length by others, whose notion, when traced and examined to the bottom, amounts, I think, to this: 'That personality is not a permanent, but a transient thing: that it lives and dies, begins and ends continually: that no one can any more remain one and the same person two moments together, than two successive moments can be one and the same moment: that our substance is indeed continually changing; but whether this be so or not, is, it seems, nothing to the purpose; since it is not substance, but consciousness alone, which constitutes personality; which consciousness, being successive, cannot be the same in any two moments, nor consequently the personality constituted by it.' And from hence it must follow, that it is a fallacy upon ourselves, to charge our present selves with anything we did ...yesterday...since our present self is not, in reality, the same with the self of yesterday, but another like self or person coming in its room, and mistaken for it; to which another self will succeed tomorrow.[30]

By severing substance from selfhood and by locating personal identity instead in consciousness, Locke had paved the way —as his critics viewed it—for a denial of the abiding self and of moral responsibility.

After lodging these charges—which are not new—Butler goes on to defend them against a possible objection that might be raised by Locke's followers. Had he not, after all, confused

Locke's theory with the interpretation given it by Collins and others? "It may be thought, perhaps," says Butler,

> that this is not a just representation of the opinion we are speaking of: because those who maintain it allow, that a person is the same as far back as his remembrance reaches.... But they cannot, consistently with themselves, mean, that the person is really the same. For it is self-evident, that the personality cannot be really the same, if, as they expressly assert, that in which it consists is not the same. And as, consistently with themselves, they cannot so...mean, that the person is *really* the same, but only that he is so in a fictitious sense.[31]

We will leave it to be considered how close Locke's theory, when pushed to this conclusion, comes to Hume's contention three years later that the "identity, which we ascribe to the mind of man, is only a fictitious one." Noting that the "chief difficulty" of Locke's theory "relates to [a person's] being the same with himself at different times," and that the "Personality...in this world or the other, must not stand on such a shifting and changeable principle," Isaac Watts's critique of Locke in 1733 suggests a similar direction.[32] Important here is Butler's belief, shared by others, that Locke had done something significant to the concept of the self.

Also important is Butler's own justification for his work. He has argued at such length against the self-in-consciousness, he tells us, because "great stress is said to be put [on] it."[33] Though Locke's theory continued to be attacked in the 1720s and 1730s, this statement in 1736 suggests that the new view was slowly beginning to gain a gradual though hard-fought acceptance.

One vehicle to such acceptance was offered by John Harris and Ephraim Chambers. Harris (ca. 1666–1719), a Boyle Lecturer in 1698, a Fellow and later Secretary of the Royal Society, and an opponent of Arbuthnot and others in the controversy over Dr. Woodward's *Essay Toward a Natural History of the Earth* (1695), published a book between 1704 and 1710 that was, at its time, "the only work of its kind in the language."[34] Harris's *Lexicon Technicum* was the first scientific encyclopedia, "a strenuous effort to gather up the latest conclusions of natural science into a single massive work."[35] In the *Lexicon,* Harris closes an account of the older question of the *"Principium Individuationis"* with a mention of "another sort of Identity" recently determined by "Mr. *Lock*":

> But there is another sort of *Identity,* which hath not been improperly called *Personal*; which I think Mr. *Lock* truly determines to consist in the *Sameness of a Rational Being*: Since by *Person* we understand an Intelligent Being, having Reason and Reflection: And since there is a *Consciousness* which always accompanies Thinking; it is that which makes every one to be that, which he calls *himself,* ... and gives him his *Personal Identity.*[36]

A decade later, while apprenticed to a well-known map-maker named Senex, Ephraim Chambers (d. 1740) planned a collection on a much larger scale than the *Lexicon Technicum,* with the expressed intent (the *DNB* tells us) of outdoing Harris. The result was *The Cyclopaedia: Or, An Universal Dictionary of Arts and Sciences* (1728) which ran through four editions by 1741 and insured Chambers's immediate election to the Royal Society. From 1728 on, the eighteenth-century reader of this extremely popular work could glance at the entry for "Identity" and discover, first, that it is an equivocal term, depending on that to which it is applied: "it being one thing, to be the same Substance; another, the same Man; and the third, the same Person." When the reader came to identity of person, he would learn that "Person stands for an intelligent Being, that reasons, and reflects, and can consider itself the same thing in different Times and Places; which it doth by that Consciousness, that is inseparable from Thinking. By this everyone is to himself, what he calls Self.... In this consists Personal *Identity*."[37] All this, of course, comes right out of Locke's chapter, as does the remainder of Chambers's entry. By including alphabetized entries in both the sciences and the arts, Chambers was literally inventing the modern encyclopedia. So it is difficult to tell what his assumptions were. In citing the criterion of consciousness, was he passing on what he saw, in 1728, as the received truth on the matter? Or was Chambers, like his rival and predecessor Harris, giving the *latest* findings on the subject? (Chambers's introduction, which provided a model for Johnson's later *Preface to the Dictionary*, seems to suggest the latter. "THRO'OUT the Whole," he asserts, "we have had a particular regard, both in the Choice of the several heads, and in dwelling...upon'em, to...opening new Tracks, new Scenes, new Vistas." Elsewhere he tells us that we can expect to find a "Multitude of Improvements in the several Parts" of knowledge "made in these last Years.")[38] In any case, the use of the new criterion in Chambers and Harris, as well as its appearance in more polite places such as *The Spectator*, helped popularize Locke's theory and increase Butler's apprehension in 1736.

Several years after Butler's warning about the great stress placed on Locke's criterion, Hume would note in his "Appendix" to the *Treatise* (1740) that "Most philosophers" now "seem inclin'd to think, that personal identity *arises* from consciousness."[39] We have moved a long way from Stillingfleet's question, over forty years before: "How comes *Person* to stand for *this*?"

Along with the critique of the substantial self and the new criterion of consciousness, a third theme emerges: the puzzles of identity. Locke is generally held to be the first to see the importance of such puzzles to the problem of personal identity. Though this needs qualification—we earlier watched Aquinas, for example, wrestle with a resurrected cannibal—Locke's consideration was certainly the most extensive to date. And in, say, the case of the man who thought he had the soul of Socrates, we have seen Locke employ his criterion to determine whether the term "same person" can be applied.

Perhaps because of the importance Locke attached to such cases, eighteenth-century authors took an interest in the puzzles of identity, and they were capable of coming up with their own. They were even more interested in some "puzzling Questions" Locke's own theory posed, particularly the possibility that the same man could, at different times, be different persons.[40] Once consciousness becomes a test of personal identity, other problems arise. Were someone's consciousness lost, for instance, he would not on Locke's principles be the "same person," though he would still be the "same man."

The possible loss or alienation of consciousness was a concern because of its bearing on moral responsibility. If it were possible for the same man to be different persons, how could that man be fairly judged, either here or in the afterlife? Or, more properly, *which* person would be judged? Such a puzzle is put to Locke by Henry Lee: "Suppose a person be decay'd in his Memory and Intellectuals, shall he not be reputed the *same* person for defect of *Consciousness*?" Lee has in fact heard of three "Persons in this Age, that have been the Honours of it, who, before they went off, were much decay'd in their Memory and Intellectuals... Dr. *Henry More*, Dr. *John Parson* Bishop of *Chester*, Dr. *Seth Ward* Bishop of *Salisbury*," all "admir'd for their incomparable Learning, Wisdom, and Piety, [who] were not very far above the state of Children before they died: Were they not therefore the *same* Persons?" Lee has his own answer to this puzzle, resolved by the substantial soul. "Surely," he tells Locke, "the *same divine* Soul which acted [in] their Bodies, as awkward as they were, the *same Principle* of all their Intellectual Operations was enough to denominate them *such*?"[41]

Collins has a similar puzzle for Clarke, though with a less comforting answer. In *An Answer to Mr. Clarke's Third Defence*, he challenges Clarke "to account for the Resurrection" on the "following Case":

> Suppose a Man lives and believes as a good Christian ought to do for forty Years, and then has a Distemper in his Body which obliterates all the Ideas lodged in the numerical individual immaterial Substance; so that on his Recovery there remains no Memory, no Consciousness of any Idea that he perceived for forty Years past. And further, suppose this numerical, individual, immaterial Substance, to get Ideas again as a young Child does, and till its Separation from the Body, leads a dissolute and debauched Life. Here on my Principles is the same Being at different times, as much two Persons as any two Men in the World are two Persons, or as the same Man mad and sober is two Persons. Now I ask him, whether or no they are two distinct Persons? If he answers, they are two distinct Persons: I ask him, how one of them can be punished eternally, and the other eternally rewarded, on the Supposition that the same numerical individual Substance is necessary to constitute the *same Person*?
>
> (p. 878)

Clarke's response to this puzzle, involving alienation of consciousness, is similar to Lee's:

> The Case you put, of a Person living well for some Years, and afterwards forgetting that he had done so, and then living for the future in all manner of Debauchery; is so far from being an *Absurdity*, as you call it, upon my Notion of Personal Identity; that, on the contrary, there is no manner of Difficulty in it. The Man is not *two Persons, as much as any two Men in the World are two Persons*; (which you declare he must be, in Consequence of *your* Principles....) But he is, I confess, (as you

add in the next Words,) *as much two Persons*, as *the same Man mad and sober is two Persons*; that is, he is *not at all two Persons*, but plainly *one and the same Person*; and shall be justly punished as his Iniquities deserve.

(p. 904)

Variations of the alienation puzzle also appear in Shaftesbury, Berkeley, Perronet, and Watts. All pick up perhaps the most frequent example employed in the debate, the madman/sober man puzzle. So does the author of *An Essay on Consciousness* (1728), who notes that "when thro' Phrenzy, or other Disorder, a Man is not Conscious of Himself... we say, *he is beside Himself*, or *is not Himself*.... So that *Consciousness* denominates *Self*, and *Self* may rightly be defined, *That which is Conscious*."[42] In defending Locke's chapter against Butler's attack, Vincent Perronet likewise puzzles in his *Second Vindication of Mr. Locke* (1738):

> Is the *Mad* Man *justly* punishable for what the *Sober* Man did? If he be not, then we must allow that something more is necessary to constitute the *same Person*... than barely being the *same Man*. He that has lost his Understanding, and the Remembrance of his Crimes, is yet the *same living Agent*, and may, I presume, be call'd the *same guilty Man*: But if he be not the *same Conscious Being*, or the *same proper Object of Punishment*, he is not in Mr. *Locke's* Phrase, the *same Person*.[43]

Berkeley shares an interest in such puzzles. In *Alciphron* (1732), Euphranor (representing Berkeley) tells Alciphron of the need to "untie the knots and answer all the objections" raised "even about human personal identity." The ensuing dialogue develops a puzzle created by Locke's theory, which Alciphron supports:

ALCIPHRON: Methinks, there is no such mystery in personal identity.

EUPHRANOR: Pray, in what do you take it to consist?

ALCIPHRON: In consciousness.

EUPHRANOR: Whatever is possible may be supposed?

ALCIPHRON: It may.

EUPHRANOR: We will suppose now (which is possible in the nature of things, and reported to be fact) that a person, through some violent accident or distemper, should fall into such a total oblivion as to lose all consciousness of his past life and former ideas. I ask, is he not still the same person?

ALCIPHRON: He is the same man, but not the same person.

Though Alciphron supports Locke's theory, Berkeley does not. And Euphranor proceeds, in an elaborate proof known as the "Gallant Officer," to argue that "personal identity doth not consist in consciousness."[44]

Another version of this puzzle involves the possibility of a deluded consciousness that appropriates thoughts and actions foreign to itself. Such a puzzle appears in the *Philosophical Essays* (1733) of Isaac Watts, who argues that if Locke's "twenty seventh chapter" were "universally received," it "would bring in endless confusions, wheresoever the word person was introduced." According to Watts, Locke's doctrine enables the madman to be not just one other person, but as many persons as he wishes:

> For if Mr. N. Lee, the tragedian in Bedlam, hath a strong impression on his fancy, that he taught Plato philosophy, then he is the same person with Socrates; or that he pleaded in the Roman senate against Mark Antony, then he is Cicero; or that he subdued Gaul ... then he is Julius Caesar; that he wrote the *Aeneids*, then he is Virgil; that he began the reformation from popery, then he is Martin Luther; and that he reigned in England at the latter end of the sixteenth century, and then he is the same person with Queen Elizabeth.

Such a case arises from "fancy imitating the act of memory."

(Hume would soon discover little difference between the two.) In this puzzle, Watts misses Locke's own dictum that a good God would not allow such a situation as "N. Lee's" to influence His decision at the Judgment (2.27.13). Like Berkeley, Butler, and others, Watts also tends to read the Lockean "consciousness" as an equivalent to "memory." As a substantialist, he fails, too, to see how *human identity* can in any way be considered an equivocal term. As he later mentions, "person and man" on his principles "are here the same." He does, however, give a critique of Locke which Johnson later admired.[45]

Watts also develops another puzzle that parallels Leibniz's criticism on the continent and Molyneux's comments in some earlier correspondence. This is a case in which moral accountability extends *beyond* consciousness and a person may be said to be (1) unconscious of his acts and (2) still responsible for them. "Suppose," says Watts, that

> *Armando* has slain his neighbour in the sight of *Martys* and *Criton*, and should be seized with such loss of memory afterward, or such distraction, as to blot out the consciousness of this action from the mind. *Armando* then would say, It was not I: But may not *Martys* and *Criton* still charge him, Thou art the murderer? May they not justly say of him, That he is guilty, and he should be put to death? Are they not as good judges of the same person as *Armando* is himself? What if *Armando* should deny the fact, as having really lost all consciousness of it? Is he not still the same person that slew his neighbour? Does not the witness of *Martys* and *Criton* declare him to be the same person? They know his body to be the same; and ... they justly infer his soul must be the same also, whatsoever *Armando's* distraction might dictate concerning himself.

Thus, Watts concludes, the work "*person*" stands for "one intelligent substance, which is always the same, whether it be or be not conscious ... of its own actions in different times and places."[46] If Locke could answer this charge, he would perhaps argue that though human laws would hang Armando the man, if he were not conscious of the murder Armando the person would not be held divinely accountable.

Locke had no such answer for William Molyneux in 1693–1694. After reading an advance copy of the new chapter he suggested, Molyneux could at first find little criticism. But a second look convinced him of a problem in 2.27.22, which argues that the "drunken man" and the "sleep walker" should not be held responsible for their acts, because they are not the same conscious persons. Though "this is true," Molyneux tells Locke, "in the Case of the Nightwalker," it is not true in the case of the drunk. "For Drunkenes is it self a Crime, and therefore no one shall alledge it in excuse of an other Crime." Drunkenness is also "a Deliberate Act which a man may easily avoid and Prevent." We therefore have a case here where moral accountability extends beyond consciousness. Though Locke cannot see what the commission of one crime while involved in another has to do with consciousness, he does admit to Molyneux that "if a man may be punish'd for any crime which he committed when drunk, whereof he is allow'd not to be conscious, it overturns my hypothesis." And when Molyneux pressed the issue home, by arguing again that drunkenness is a sober, voluntary decision, Locke seemingly relented and agreed that the "want of consciousness ought not to be presum'd in favour of the drunkard."[47]

A far more speculative puzzle is the possibility of the transfer of consciousness from one subject to another. Here we again have a situation in which the same man can be different persons. Locke demonstrates this highly improbable situation, we recall, with his instance of the prince and the cobbler in 2.27.15. Should "the Soul of a Prince," says Locke, "carrying with it the consciousness of the Prince's past Life, enter and inform the Body of a Cobler as soon as deserted by his own Soul, every one sees, he would be the same Person with the Prince....But who would say it was the same Man?"

This puzzle shows up in a slightly altered form in *Spectator* no. 578, the paper that informs us that there "has been very great Reason...for the learned World to endeavour at settling what it was that might be said to compose, *personal Identity*." Immediately after this comment, the author (perhaps Eustace Budgell) discusses the problem of personal identity and locates it in Locke's theory. "Mr. *Lock*, after having premised that the Word *Person* properly signifies a thinking intelligent Being that has Reason and Reflection, and can consider it self as it self; concludes, That it is Consciousness alone, and not an Identity of Substance, which makes this personal Identity or Sameness." After further quoting from Locke's chapter, the author tells us that "I was mightily pleased with a Story in some Measure applicable to this Piece of Philosophy, which I read the other Day in *The Persian Tales*."

He follows with an abridgment of the story of King Fadlallah and the dervish, a wild tale of disembodied consciousness, reanimated bodies, and shifting and mistaken identities. As in the case of Locke's prince whose consciousness informs the body of a cobbler, we have here a situation in which the same *man* is a different *person*. The story centers on the dervish's strange *"Power of reanimating a dead Body, by flinging my own Soul into it."* The dervish conveys the secret of this power to the unfortunate king, who attempts it immediately by leaving his own body and informing the body of a deer, whereby the dervish instantly flings his consciousness into the body of the king, makes love to the king's wife, and orders all the deer in the kingdom killed. But the king escapes, by entering the body of a dead nightingale and becoming the queen's favorite bird. When her lapdog dies, the king leaves the body of the nightingale and assumes the shape of the dog. The queen is, of course, grieved over the death of her favorite bird; and when the dervish, to comfort her, leaves the king's body and re-animates the nightingale to make it sing again, the king "immediately recovered his own Body, and running to the Cage with utmost Indignation, twisted off the Neck of the false Nightingale." [48] As *The Spectator* reports it, such a story, hinging on the possibility of the same man being a different person, is made more probable by Mr. Locke's new "Piece of Philosophy."

If philosophy or literature fails to invent such puzzles, life provides them. What do we do with the case Richard Burthogge reports in 1694, of "a *Child*" who had a "*double* Body, that is to say double Breast, and double Head, and *proper* feeling of all parts"? [49] Or with the account, in the 1700 edition of the popular manual *Aristotle's Masterpiece*, of "a man" who "hath two Heads [and] four Hands"? [50] Such stories affirm a more recent assertion that Siamese twins tend to "challenge our individuality, along with the distinction between self and other upon which that individuality depends." [51] This is also true of the Hungarian twins who toured Europe with their father and captured the imagination of London in the summer of 1708. Here, as the handbill advertising them indicates, is a real case of two persons in the same body:

> At Mr. John Pratt's, at the Angel in Cornhil ... are to be seen two Girls, who are one of the greatest Wonders in Nature that ever was seen, being Born with their Backs fastn'd to each other, and the Passages of their Bodies are both one way. These Children are very Handsome and Lusty, and Talk three different Languages; they are going into the 7th year of their Age. Those who see them, may very well say, they have seen a Miracle, which may pass for the 8th Wonder of the World. [52]

Like *The Spectator* and *Aristotle's Masterpiece*, the case of the twins reflects a popular interest in such puzzles. "Here is the sight of two girls joined together at the back," Swift wrote

Stearne in June 1708, "which, in the newsmonger's phrase, causes a great many speculations; and raises abundance of questions in divinity, law, and physic."[53] Many such speculations appeared in a series of puzzle questions addressed to *The British Apollo* the same summer. Given the nature of the case, a number of these questions, as well as the meager and often humorous attempts at answering them, touched on the problem of personal identity. "Since the Twins have some Parts in common to both," one question puts it, "how can they rise from the Dead with the *same* individual Bodies?" Another asks, "Whether each of the Twins brought into England, hath a distinct Soul, or whether one informs both?" Still another asks about moral accountability: "If one of the monstrous Twins lately brought over should commit a Crime worthy of Death, how should it be punished?" (The *Apollo* answers that both twins should be punished by death only if the one could have prevented the crime of the other; otherwise, it is better that the guilty go unpunished than that the innocent one suffer.) As the handbill indicates, the twins also seem to have been attractive, prompting questions about their possible maturity and marriage. One questioner asks "Whether, if any marry one of the two Children, when grown up, who are so monstrously conjoin'd, he be guilty of incest?" (The *Apollo* answers that in the case of the twins, "the forementioned Sin is unavoidable.") Still another asks: "Could a Man marry the Twins, and not be guilty of Polygamy?" "If the Meaning of Polygamy," the *Apollo* responds, "is to have more Wives than one, and the Twins signifie more Women than one, certainly it is Polygamy to marry the Twins."[54] Perhaps a real Lockean might have asked, "Do the twins have the same consciousness of their apparently common parts?" Nevertheless, this strange case and the puzzles of identity generated by Locke's theory find a special place in *The Memoirs of Scriblerus.*

4

On a "Metaphysical Goe-cart"
Responses, Satiric and Otherwise

> When You have set your Self in your
> Metaphysical Goe-cart, in order to step sure,
> You walk too Slow to rid any Ground.
> *Matthew Prior to John Locke, 1721*

As *The Spectator* suggests, talk about identity and consciousness was not confined to the metaphysical arena. The discussion enjoyed a wider popularity in a country where, in
Hume's words, "all the abstruser sciences are study'd with
a peculiar ardour and application."[1] Throughout the early
eighteenth century, the Clarke-Collins controversy, for instance, seems almost to have had a life of its own. This popularity was perhaps due not only to the interest in the issues it
raised but to the reputation of Samuel Clarke, regarded in his
own time as "the foremost of living English philosophers."[2]
(Years after Clarke's death, the great physiologist Robert
Whytt would point to the pamphlets against Collins, where
"Perspecuity...and sound Philosophy are happily united."[3]
And Samuel Johnson, who may have drawn on these same
pamphlets in *Rasselas*, would call Clarke "the most complete
literary character 'England' ever produced.")[4] In any case, if
a reader in the 1720s did not wish to lumber through the lengthy
pages of the Clarke-Collins dispute itself, he could consult a
handy, thirty-six-page abridgment prepared by John Maxwell and published in 1727. A copy of this later surfaces in the
sale catalogue of Arbuthnot's books.[5] In the 1730s, Collins's

use of Locke's theory becomes a central target of Butler's critique. And two years later, while defending Locke against Butler's charges, Vincent Perronet is still at pains in 1738 to extricate Locke's theory from the "absurd and wicked Use" of it in "an Answer to Dr. *Clarke's* third Defense." [6]

As an index of the continuing debate over Locke's theory —the debate Hume would mention in 1739—we can note several others who contribute to the discussion or comment on it. In *A Treatise of the Hypochondriack and Hysteric Passions* (second edition, 1730), for example, Dr. Bernard Mandeville assures worried patients that the "Resurrection of the same Person" must "necessarily include the Restitution of Consciousness." [7] Mandeville alludes to an issue that would not go away. Early critics attacked Locke's view here. Others followed suit. For instance, in a sermon at Oxford in 1719, Winch Holdsworth claimed that Locke's concept of identity-of-consciousness made the Resurrection impossible—a charge that prompted Catherine Trotter to come out of retirement (after raising a large family) and write *A Letter to Dr. Holdsworth, in Vindication of Mr. Locke* (1726). [8] Holdsworth countered with *A Defence of the Doctrine of the Resurrection of the Same Body. In ... which the Character, Writings, and Religious Principles of Mr. Lock are Distinctly Considered* (1727). Two years before this second attack of Holdsworth's—which is often more of an assassination than a consideration—Henry Felton delivered another Oxford sermon which, the *DNB* says, "excited considerable attention" at the time. Felton was a highly popular preacher, and his *Resurrection of the same Numerical Body ... In which Mr. Lock's Notions of Personality and Identity are confuted* (1725) was evidently a success. It ran through three published editions—two the same year and the third in 1733, when a sequel appeared, upholding the substantial view of personal identity and attacking Locke's chapter.

In a preface to the second edition of the 1725 sermon,

Felton mentions "the Controversy between the most Learned Dr. Stillingfleet...and Mr. Lock."[9] This reference, nearly thirty years after that controversy, reminds us that the earliest extended discussion of Locke's theory (1696–1699) still continued to be known. Irvin Ehrenpreis has argued that the themes alone of this debate were "in the air for decades." Felton supports that claim, as does Isaac Watts, who refers frequently in 1733 to the "warm dispute...between Mr. Locke and Bishop Stillingfleet." Bayle's *Dictionnaire* (fourth edition, 1730) also cites *"la fameuse Dispute du Doctour Stillingfleet & de Monsieur Locke,"* and the 1737 English version of that dictionary notes that the same debate has "made much noise in England."[10]

That this noise reverberated not simply in the polemical but also in the polite world is suggested by a number of works, including a strange piece by Matthew Prior in 1721, titled *A Dialogue Between Mr: John Lock and Seigneur de Montaigne.* In this work, which Pope read in manuscript and "thought very good," a fictionalized Montaigne tells Locke of the dispute "between You and Stillingfleet" and accuses him of jumping on a "Metaphysical Goe-cart" that takes him nowhere.[11] In questioning the inherent value of such disputes—a point with which the Scriblerians might agree—Montaigne also castigates Locke for his theory of personal identity and larger concern with consciousness. Humorously paraphrasing Locke at one point, Montaigne comments: "The Identity of the same Man consists in a participation of the same continued life by constantly fleeting particles of Matter in Succession Vitally United to the same Organized Body. So that an Embryo is not a Person of One and Twenty. Ismael is not Socrates, Pilate is not St. Austin. Who Questions any thing of this, good Mr. Lock...?" While satirizing the Locke-Stillingfleet dispute and Locke's theory, Montaigne also takes in the famed rational parrot. "You tell Us," he says, "That Prince Maurice had an Old Parot in Brazil who Spoke and Asked and Answered Questions like a reasonable Creature, who told the Prince he knew him to be a General, that he himself belonged to a Portuguese, that he came from Marinnan, and that his imployment was to keep the Chickens. Now who ever believed this but Sir William Temple and your Self?" As such passages suggest, Prior has little patience with Locke. The tone throughout is hostile, the satire unremitting. Locke, Prior claims, has "cut" the soul "up like an Anatomy." The mind (his Montaigne adds) should not always "be imploy'd only on it self, but upon other things." Locke, however, is always thinking and talking about himself. When Locke protests that "You, the loosest of Writers, have no great respect for my close way of Reasoning," Montaigne replies: "Really, Mr: Lock, I should flatter You, if I said I had." Indeed, "while you wrote" the *Essay concerning Human Understanding*, "you were only thinking that You thought"; for

> You, and Your understanding are the *Personae Dramatis*, and the whole amounts to no more than a Dialogue between John and Lock.
>
> > As I walked by my Self
> > And talked to my self,
> > And my Self said unto me.[12]

We moderns might find it surprising for Montaigne, of all writers, to be characterized as scolding Locke for thinking and talking only about himself. Montaigne thought and talked a good deal about *himself*, so what separates Locke's concerns from his? One way of approaching this might be to bring in Pope's comment on the *Dialogue*, which takes as central what initially appears in Prior to be a minor distinguishing point. The *Dialogue*, Pope said, shows Locke's "most regular" and Montaigne's "very loose way of thinking."[13] Pope's distinction seems to rest on different styles of argumentation: Montaigne's randomness versus Locke's rigor. And Pope may have been evoking this element of the contrast when he later claimed that

> As drives the storm, at any door I knock,
> And house with Montagne now, or now with Lock.[14]

Pope's distinction is more involved than this, however, as is Prior's. In a conversation with Joseph Spence, Pope certainly had Montaigne in mind when noting that there "is a great number of exceeding good writers among the French," though they "don't *think so closely* or speak so clearly as Locke." Here, as in the statement on Prior's *Dialogue*, the difference Pope perceives is not simply in mode of argument but "way of thinking." Locke *thinks* differently—more "closely" —than Montaigne. Put another way: it is one thing to think about oneself, another to think, in terms as precise as possible, about *how* one thinks about oneself. This new way of thinking about thinking, Locke's close attention to consciousness and "the *Perception of the Operations of our own Minds*," is what separates his approach from that of earlier writers.[15] It is also what prompts Prior's criticism about Locke's preoccupation with himself—that "Dialogue between John and Lock" in which "You were only thinking that You thought." In the wake of Locke's *Essay*, Richard Burthogge and others had called for more attention to the "Notion of *Consciousness*" and "the *Way* and Manner [it] Arises."[16] Prior wants less attention, for he sees the subject and approach as solipsistic.

For us, another question might be why Montaigne, in Prior's *Dialogue*, would be disturbed by Locke's theory of personal identity. After all, Montaigne's *Essays*—most notably, "Of the Inconstancy of Our Actions" and "The Apology for Raymond Sebond"—have been seen by some to advance a distinctly modern view of the self, even "the dissolution of the personality into an assemblage of multiple facets, with the consequent impossibility of pinning any single personality down."[17] In having Montaigne attack Locke's consideration of the soul Prior provides a significant objection to this view. And here the historical Montaigne would agree. Though he everywhere emphasizes the apparent flux of experience— a point not lost on Pope—Montaigne also knows that the "Soul...is the sole and sovereign Mistress of our Condition."[18] A recent commentator is correct in saying that Montaigne "never seems to doubt that in the world of becoming the [substantial] self exists to be known, or rather to be sought through the very flux and mutability that obscure it."[19] A century after Montaigne, Locke does not have the same assurance—a point that underlies Prior's critique, as it had Stillingfleet's.

These later references to the Locke-Stillingfleet exchange were not the last. In 1819, nearly a century after Prior's *Dialogue*, Coleridge speaks of Locke's "controversy with the Bishop of Worcester" and argues that the writings of the "great Stillingfleet" constitute "some of the finest works of philosophy for that period"—works, he adds, which "were not merely put down at once as trash out of fashion, but it was said that Stillingfleet had died of a broken heart in consequence of his defeat by Locke."[20]

Coleridge's last contention here is doubtful—Stillingfleet was, after all, a very old man—though the poet's comments do point to the staying power of some concerns of the early controversy. That Stillingfleet was dismissed "at once" also needs to be qualified. A contemporary, Thomas Hearne, recorded in 1734 that "it hath been allowed by all, that Locke had much the advantage of the Bishop."[21] Yet Stillingfleet was by no means alone in his doubts about the implications of the *Essay*, particularly in the hands of the Deists. (As Berkeley indicated in 1707–1708, there were other "Stillingfleetians" around.)[22] Writing in an age when, in the words of one Locke supporter, "so many hands" were "employed, just at the same time, to Attack and Batter this Essay," Stillingfleet was believed to be a considerable foe of Locke.[23] As contemporary accounts suggest, he was also regarded as a respected thinker in his own right. In *The Dispensary* (1699), for instance, Sir Samuel Garth remarks:

> Sooner than I'll from vow'd Revenge desist,
> His *Holiness* shall turn a Quietist.
>
> . . . .
>
> Faith stand unmov'd thro' *Stillingfleet's* Defence
> And *Lock* for Mystery abandon Sense.[24]

A year earlier, in *A Free but Modest Censure on the late Controversial Writings ... of the Lord Bishop of Worcester and Mr. John Locke* (1698), an anonymous writer characterizes Stillingfleet as "one who dives into Men as well as Books" and also commends his "accurate anatomizing" of Locke. For Stillingfleet "shews that this Gentleman hath introduced *New Terms* to unsettle the knowledg [*sic*] of things, and amuse the minds of the unwary.... To which I will add what I have lately observed my self out of his *Essay of Human Understanding*." According to this writer in 1698, Stillingfleet has already won the debate; and "others agree with me in it, that the Reverend Bishop hath all along proved that Mr. *Lock contradicts himself*" and that he also has "an inclination to overthrow some of the chiefest Articles of the *Christian Faith*." This must be the case, the author claims, when those who support "sober Philosophy and Orthodox Divinity" support Stillingfleet's position, while "Persons of loose Principles, Scepticks, and Deists, applaud [Locke's] undertakings, and are his humble admirers."[25]

This last point, indicating the Deists' support of Locke in the controversy with Stillingfleet, is interesting; for it may also connect two strange bedfellows, Sir Richard Blackmore and Dr. Jonathan Swift. Blackmore was on friendly terms with Locke, who seems to have appreciated Sir Richard's poetry.[26] Nonetheless, in *A Satyr Against Wit* (1699), written shortly after Stillingfleet's death, Blackmore laments the damage being done the bishop by the "leud Sons of Wit":

> Horror and Shame! What would the Madmen have?
> They dig up learned *Bernard's* peaceful Grave.
> The Sacred-Urn of famous *Stillingfleet*,
> We see prophan'd by the leud Sons of Wit.[27]

The second couplet is often thought to be directed at Blackmore's chief enemy, Sir Samuel Garth. Yet, as the above passage from Garth's *Dispensary* indicates, Stillingfleet is there treated favorably. In the reference to the "Sons of Wit" debasing the "Sacred-Urn" of Stillingfleet, could Blackmore instead have had in mind those "Persons of loose Principles, Scepticks, and Deists" mentioned by the pamphlet the year before?

Whatever the case, Jonathan Swift certainly draws this connection several years later, in *Remarks upon a Book, Intitled, The Rights of the Christian Church* (1707). In this work, Swift mentions Tindal's use of "the refined Way of Speaking... introduced by Mr. *Locke*" and the author's derisive treatment of Stillingfleet. Swift also notes Tindal's misapplication of "Bishop STILLINGFLEET'S *Vindication of the Doctrine of the Trinity*." While citing this first pamphlet of the Locke-Stillingfleet controversy, Swift takes a sharp turn in defending Stillingfleet's memory against Tindal's attack:

> Upon which Account I shall say nothing of that great Instance of [Tindal's] Candour and Judgment in relation to Dr. *Stillingfleet*, who ... is High-Church and Jacobite, took the Oaths of Allegiance to save him from the Gallows and subscribed to the Articles only to keep this Preferment: Whereas the Character of that Prelate is universally known to have been directly the Reverse, of what this Writer gives him.[28]

Whether Swift himself was a Stillingfleetian will be reserved for later, though the answer in this instance seems clear. Important here is the sheer pervasiveness, hitherto unrecognized, of the early eighteenth-century discussion of identity, conducted in a wide range of different quarters, philosophical, theological, and literary. From the Locke-Stillingfleet exchange of 1696–1699 to the Butler-Perronet debate of 1736–1738, Locke's theory generated new controversies while older ones continued to be mentioned and known. When Hume claimed that *"personal identity"* had indeed become "so great a question" these "late years in *England*," he knew what he was talking about.[29]

Given the extent of the debate and Swift's acquaintance with the Locke-Stillingfleet exchange and other controversies over Locke's theory—including the Clarke-Collins rift, as Part III will suggest—it is perhaps not surprising that the larger discussion could play a part in some major works. We have observed, for instance, Watts's picture of Nat Lee in Bedlam, claiming on Locke's grounds to be any person he wants to be, including Queen Elizabeth. Michael DePorte has found a similar (if more submerged) critique of Locke's theory, thirty years earlier, in *A Tale of a Tub*. If consciousness constitutes identity, isn't a person whoever he believes he is? When a madman is *not himself*, whom does he become? These questions and others are raised in *A Tale* and in a work Swift may have known, James Carkesse's *Lucida Intervalla* (1679), possibly the first book of English poetry published by a current resident of a mental hospital. Carkesse, who dubs himself "The Doctors Patient Extraordinary," likes to identify that self with different persons—including Jesus Christ—and different roles, at different times. He is now a soldier, now a priest—

> From *Finnes-burrough*, to *Bedlam* I am come,
> To be a *Sober man*, not Act mad *Tom*:
> My name is *James*, not *Nokes*, and yet an *Actor*;

> But now, *Mad Devil*, seek another *Factor*:
> I am a Minister of God's holy Word,
> Have taken up the *Gown*, laid down the *Sword*.

Now a servant of Apollo:

> Thus the Poet did Write and Talke,
>   At *Bedlam* clad in *Freese*;
> Where his Pen and Ink, it was *Chalk*;
>   Boards, Paper; and Diet, *Cheese*.[30]

As DePorte sees it, Carkesse, unknowingly, and Swift, knowingly, address an issue Locke avoided in the chapter on identity: "to what extent do madmen actively contrive new identities? It was this aspect of the relationship of consciousness to madness which most interested Swift."[31]

The issue of identity and delusion might also say something about a later Swift work in which the narrator wants to become a horse.[32] Whether or not we can draw these lines between that work and the contemporary discussion, other connections are there. As Colie and Ehrenpreis have argued, the Locke-Stillingfleet debate in particular provides a possible source, nearly thirty years later, for the "ape-man-horse seesaw" in *Gulliver's Travels*.[33] There are other teasing allusions in the *Travels* to the debate over Locke's theory and the theory itself. At one point in Book 4, for example, Gulliver tells us that after he was caught sleeping without his clothes, his Houyhnhnm master "asked me the Meaning of what his Servant had reported; that I was not the same Thing when I slept as I appeared to be at other times." Could this be an ironic literalization of "Socrates waking" and "Socrates sleeping" (2.27.19) who appear, at least in the eyes of Locke's critics, not to be the same person?[34] That Swift and his friends were elsewhere interested in such questions is suggested by their use, in *The Memoirs of Scriblerus*, of Locke's theory of identity and the current debate surrounding it.

Part Three

Locke and the Scriblerians

5

Of Controversy and Conviviality, and a Pedant's Progress

They make a great noise about this individuality: how a
man is conscious to himself that he is the same Individual
he was twenty years ago.
The Scriblerus Club

The Memoirs of Scriblerus owe their existence to a group who constituted, in Cowper's words, the "most celebrated collection of clever fellows this country ever saw."[1] Much about the Scriblerus Club remains shadowy, but Kerby-Miller has admirably pieced together what details are available. We know that the club was made up of Swift, Arbuthnot, Pope, Parnell, and Gay, along with the Lord High Treasurer, the Earl of Oxford. We know too that the actual meetings of the group, which began in 1713, lasted only a few short months (though these meetings would leave their imprint on certain members of the club, particularly Pope and Swift, for years to come). Something of the spirit of the original meetings is suggested by the Scriblerians' rhymed invitations to their most distinguished colleague, Oxford, who is advised at one point:

> For Frolick Mirth give ore affairs of State,
> To night be happy, be to morrow great.
>
> (p. 353)

In the convivial atmosphere of these meetings, *The Memoirs* took shape as the cornerstone of an ambitious program of attack on intellectual pride and folly, a program that would produce *Gulliver's Travels* and *The Dunciad*. Any critical assessment of *The Memoirs* must take this larger satiric context into account. In exploring the Scriblerians' reaction to what they call the "great noise" over "this Individuality," it would help first, then, to review the scope of the work, its relation to some other satires of its kind, and its direction and ends.

Cast in the form of a pseudobiography of Martinus Scriblerus, eminent pedant, learned commentator on *The Dunciad*, and noted author of *The Art of Sinking* and other published matter, *The Memoirs* satirize what Pope and his friends perceived to be gross misapplications of the human intellect, above all, the type of mentality that "convert[s] every Trifle into a serious thing" and reduces all to system (p. 129). In creating "a full character who might embody mind in the process of self-destruction,"[2] the Scriblerians portray in Martinus's story a veritable pedant's progress. We observe Martinus's glorious ancestry in the pedants of the past as well as the strange prodigies that attend his birth (owls are found frolicking in his play crib); his early childhood, which prompts a learned "Dissertation upon Play-things" and subjects Martinus to his father Cornelius's program of education, a plan that proves as disastrous to the boy's welfare as Walter Shandy's later *Tristra-poedia*; Martinus's training in the old scholastic forms; his advanced work in anatomy and criticism (the former ending in a midnight escapade with a farting corpse); his later investigations of human psychology and the state of the soul, which bring a letter from a fictionalized Anthony Collins giving *his* side of the debate with Clarke; and, finally, Martinus's incredible marriage to what the eighteenth century would have simply called a "monster."

Such, in outline, is a work scholars have located in a broad tradition ranging from such earlier attacks on pedantry as *The Praise of Folly* to such contemporary pieces as Swift's *Tale of a Tub* and the satires on Bentley, Woodward, and "modernism" in general by William King and the Christ Church wits.[3] Through such features as a loose-jointed structure, a variety of topics, and a relentless attack on the *philosophus gloriosus*, *The Memoirs* also participate in the rich tradition of Menippean satire, stretching from Burton's *Anatomy of Melancholy* (and a host of other Renaissance works) back to Petronius, Lucian, and Varro.[4] The papers may draw, too, on a closely related classical type, evoked in a comment of Pope's to Joseph Spence. Some years before their publication, Pope told Spence that *The Memoirs* contained a "Deipnosophy" that "consisted of disputes on ridiculous tenets of all sorts."[5] This segment did not, however, surface in the first edition in 1741 and has never since been found. (Judging from Pope's statement and the sections of *The Memoirs* we do have, the segment would probably have satirized the kind of debate we have been discussing here and have raised the question of whether any controversy ultimately settles anything.) Nevertheless, Pope's comment, along with the group's invitations to Oxford, point to an aspect of *The Memoirs* that has gone unnoticed and to a tradition that includes Petronius's dinner with Trimalchio, as well as Macrobius's *Saturnalia*, Athenaeus's *Deipnosophists*, and Plutarch's *Quaestiones*. This is what might be called the "deipnosophical" dimension of the book.

A look at an earlier work in this tradition, by Athenaeus of Naucratis (ca. A.D. 230), may help our understanding of this dimension of *The Memoirs* and the Scriblerians' approach to the contemporary controversy over Locke. Titled *The Deipnosophists* or *The Scholars at Banquet*, Athenaeus's book employs a *cena* setting characteristic of the type. The work purports to be a record of a dinner conversation at the house of a wealthy Roman named Larensis, who has "summoned as [his] guests the men of his time most learned in their several branches of knowledge." Larensis's guests arrive for dinner and proceed "with the utmost critical, even Socratic, acumen" to discuss an incredible range of topics. The result, Athenaeus declares, is a "delightful feast of reason."[6]

Though *The Deipnosophists* is too diffuse to characterize easily, it does have some striking features. First, there is the ever-present element of the *ludus*, the game, as each guest adds his share of wit and erudition to the flow of jokes, puns, and parodies that enlivens the banquet. Second, in the heterogeneity of its subjects and the variety of its style, the work exemplifies the older notion of *satura* as a "medley" or "object of mixed nature."[7] This second feature of *The Deipnosophists* points to a third, its connection with Menippean satire. At one juncture in the banquet, Larensis turns to his "Fellow Dogs" and toasts our "ancestor, Varro, surnamed the Menippean" (2:229). Menippus himself, who gave his name to Varro's lost satires, was reportedly a Cynic. It is perhaps fitting, then, that the most vocal of Larensis's guests is Cynulcus, a Cynic, who directs continual outbursts against an assorted group of philosophers, grammarians, quibblers, and pedants. After a long discourse by Myrtilus *grammaticus*, Cynulcus quotes Heraclitus—"Much learning teaches not how to possess wisdom"—and then asks the learned grammarian, "What, really, is the use of all these names, you pedant—more likely to obstruct than to instruct your hearers?" (6:289). Elsewhere we find Cynulcus fuming against the word chasers or the philosophers in the Lyceum, who are

> thin, worthless starvelings—declaring that 'this thing has no being because it is becoming, and what is becoming cannot yet be said to have become; nor, supposing that it once had being, can that which is now becoming be, for nothing that is not, is.'

"What all this means," Cynulcus exclaims, "not Apollo himself could understand" (1:427). At such moments, Cynulcus assumes a classic stance of the Menippean satirist, that of "overwhelming his pedantic targets with an avalanche of their own jargon."[8] There is a potential paradox, however, in any satire on sham learning. A modern commentator points out that Cynulcus's own "quotations from a vast number of writers" show him "to be as widely read as any of the professional grammarians" he attacks.[9] Indeed, after one of Cynulcus's learned diatribes another guest looks at him and exclaims, "books have turned your life upside-down" (7:95–97). The guest identifies the implicit trap. How does one attack a pedant without becoming a pedant? How does one satirize a squabbler without entering into the squabble itself? These are problems the Scriblerians also face, in their humorous critique of the Lockean controversy.

The Deipnosophists does not provide a source, per se, for the Scriblerus papers. The work and its tradition do, however, offer a perspective on *The Memoirs* we otherwise might not have. We recall the Scriblerians' invitations to Oxford to an evening of "Frolick Mirth." If we add that the group regularly met "formally to dine and 'sit upon' their project," we can see the Scriblerians themselves engaging in their own "Banquets of the Learned" at the time when *The Memoirs* were first being conceived.[10] Though these original deipnosophies go unmentioned in the work Pope later prepared for press, they left their mark. Athenaeus tells us that "every symposium can be better understood by comparison and contrast with others" (2:327). At one point in *The Memoirs*, Cornelius Scriblerus and his "learned companions" sit down to a "moderate Supper" and get into an immediate argument about the dining practices of the ancients. Elsewhere, we hear of young Martinus's precocity at his father's frequent symposia. Behind these and other activities of the pedants, however, there is always the suggested (if shadowy) presence of another gathering, which frequently took place at

Arbuthnot's quarters in St. James. At this meeting, amid continual eruptions of wit and laughter, the Scriblerians exchange information, sport with their pedantic targets, and thoroughly enjoy what Pope would call a "Feast of Reason and the Flow of Soul."[11]

This Scriblerian *cena* suggests itself at least two ways in the later, published work. The first is in the collaborative nature of *The Memoirs*, reflected in the sheer range of subjects— identity is only one of several issues considered—and in the diffuseness of the style. (Whenever the reader begins to find "any one Chapter dull," we are told, "the style will be immediately changed in the next" [p. 94].) This variety (*satura*), in subject and style, and the qualities mentioned earlier link the work not simply to the deipnosophy but to the larger tradition of Menippean satire.

The second deipnosophical element in *The Memoirs* is the *ludus*, which pervades the work. We observe it in the playful pseudo-serious, mock-scholarly language ("I am not ignorant of what Columnesius affirms"); in the wild exercises in Scriblerian chop-logic, the art of taking an absurd position and making it appear plausible; and in the collective and convivial nature of the wit, evident in the catalogues, parodies, and jokes that abound. The *ludus* also reveals itself in the frequent word games and verbal transformations, where the Scriblerians use the same term with contrary meanings, or conflate one realm of reference with another, or take a mental abstraction and literalize it. This kind of play produces, for example, an unheard-of connection between sex and logic— in Crambe's theory of syllogisms:

> He suppos'd that a Philosopher's brain was like a great Forest, where Ideas rang'd like animals of several kinds; that those Ideas copulated and engender'd Conclusions; that when those of different Species copulate, they bring forth monsters or absurdities; that the *Major* is the male, the *Minor*

the female, which copulate by the Middle Term, and engender the Conclusion.

(p. 121)

The *ludus* is important to a larger understanding of *The Memoirs* and to our present purposes, for it colors the Scriblerians' approach to intellectual topics in general and the world of eighteenth-century controversy in particular. One scholar has lamented the fact that a group of highly talented persons with, presumably, better things to do sat around and played "literary games."[12] Yet it is precisely this element of *ludus* that enables the Scriblerians to do so much. For one thing, it helps them avoid a danger common to all those who write Menippean satire—or write about it. This is the trap Cynulcus tumbles into when he loses perspective on his pedantic subjects and becomes what he attacks. The game allows the Scriblerians to get involved in the activities of their satiric targets and simultaneously to maintain the guise of a controlled and critical distance. The *ludus* also helps, with other factors, to create the complex tone we meet in the Scriblerians' treatment of the current controversy over identity: a tone simultaneously engaged and disengaged, involved in the fracas yet somehow outside it.

A further point needs to be made about this Scriblerian game. It was a *serious* one. As Charles Kerby-Miller points out, the group did not plan *The Memoirs* simply to satirize current scholarship; the Scriblerians also hoped to produce a work of "significant value to the progress of learning in their day."[13] In one episode, Cornelius plans (on the authority of Pliny) the immediate removal of young Martinus's spleen. To save the boy, Mrs. Scriblerus calls in Cornelius's brother Albertus. An emblem of sanity in a world of madness—like Lord Munodi in *Gulliver's Travels*[14]—Albertus is described as "a discreet man, sober in his opinions, clear of Pedantry, and knowing enough both in books and in the world, to preserve a due regard for whatever was useful or excellent, whether ancient or modern." If Albertus "had not always the authority," we are told, "he had at least the art, to divert Cornelius from many extravagancies" (p. 113). Albertus's approach to his brother Cornelius is analogous to the Scriblerians' approach to the intellectual concerns of their time. They seek in *The Memoirs* not to attack learning itself but to use their art to comment on its direction and check its "extravagancies."

Kenneth Maclean has noted the Scriblerians' "interested antipathy for philosophy."[15] This is a good place for us to start, since one problem in evaluating their use of the Lockean debate is the question of tone. The deipnosophical dimension helps to account for a simultaneous involvement and detachment in approaching such issues and for the ways the Scriblerians play with the language and themes of the debate. But other complications arise. Consider, for example, this train of events: convinced that "*Logick* and *Metaphysick*," being "*Polemical* Arts, could no more be learned alone, than Fencing or Cudgel-playing" (p. 118), Cornelius Scriblerus chooses a worthy companion, Conradus Crambe, for his son Martinus. Under Cornelius's careful instruction, the boys learn Aristotle's predicaments. And when the boys are ready to "exercise the Weapons *Logick* had put into their hands," they debate the thesis of whether "the Innate Desire of the knowledge of Metaphysics was the cause of the Fall of Adam," in order to find it—"*affirm'd*" (p. 123).

This thesis perhaps reflects the Scriblerians' position in the traditional quarrel, instigated by Plato, between poet and philosopher, rhetorician and dialectician. (As Paul Kristeller wryly remarks, since "the rhetorician offers to speak and write about everything, and the philosopher tries to think about everything, they have always been rivals in their claim to provide a universal training of the mind.")[16] More specifically, it reveals a complex of attitudes about the uses of controversy in the search for truth, about the old scholastic system and the ontological terminology that made the substantial vision of the personality possible, indeed, about the value of speculative philosophy itself. To understand the Scriblerians' approach to the contemporary controversy over identity, we need to look briefly at these interlocking elements.

"It is an odd Humour in some Men," one contemporary controversialist complains, "to cry down all Books that look towards *Polemicks*" and to "disparage this period of Time we are cast into by saying, it is an *Age of Controversies*." Though this author and others would continue to urge the need for polemical controversy to settle important questions, there were some who disagreed.[17] Sir William Temple, for one, believed that such "captious cavils about words" had done learning more harm than good. Locke condemned the universities in particular—places where "we learn not to Live, but to Dispute"—for breeding such contentiousness; and Addison and others would follow suit.[18] One point frequently lodged against such squabbles is their pettiness. ("Surely, learned men will not quarrel about trifles!" one of William King's characters exclaims. "Oh! Madam, rather than any thing," she is told.)[19] Another, more serious charge is that such controversies more often than not serve the purposes of pride or self-justification rather than their stated aim, the disinterested pursuit of truth. "What *Tully* says of war," another contemporary remarks, "may be applied to disputing[:] it should be always so managed as to remember that the end of it is *peace*; but generally true disputants are like true sportsmen, their whole delight is in the pursuit; and a disputant no more cares for truth than the sportsman for the hare."[20] The Scriblerians, individually and collectively, agree with such sentiments (in theory at least, if not always in practice). In a sermon "On the Trinity," for instance, Swift tells us: "Let any Man but consider, when he hath a Controversy with another, although his Cause be ever so unjust, although the World be against him, how blinded he is by the Love of himself, to believe that Right is Wrong, and Wrong is Right, when it maketh for his own Advantage." In *An Essay on Criticism*, *The Dunciad*, and his correspondence, Pope similarly complains about the self-delusion, the anger, and the lack of charity shown by those who *"plague with Dispute"*; and Arbuthnot makes the same points in a late Scriblerian piece on the subject, a mock proposal published in 1731 and titled *A Brief Account of John Ginglicutt's Treatise Concerning the Altercation or Scolding of the Ancients*. This work ironically promises help to the polemical "geniuses which are daily rising in my native country" and even offers them an extraordinary discount: "The price of the book" is "ten shillings, one half to be paid down; only the polemical writers on each side shall have one copy gratis; and my cousin Ginglicutt have two."[21]

The twisting of the facts to suit one's own system or ends, the prideful display of knowledge for its own sake, the lack of charity, the anger and the pettiness—all are central motifs of the consideration of the *"Polemical* Arts" in *The Memoirs of Scriblerus*. We observe these strands not simply in Martinus's and Crambe's demonstration of the weapons of logic but everywhere else in the work. Cornelius Scriblerus, we hear, "reckon'd it a point of honour never to be vanquish'd in a dispute; from which quality he acquir'd the Title of the *Invincible Doctor*" (p. 125). And from beginning to end, the book gives us one squabble after another on any number of topics. (Perhaps the only point not up for debate is the spelling of Crambe's name—though even this "may be," he tells us, "some dispute to posterity.") At worst, the Scriblerians' involvement in the topical details of various contemporary debates—including that over Locke's theory—has led to the charge from Johnson on of the work's inaccessibility. At the best, however, their treatment of current controversies—the Clarke-Collins exchange, for instance—usually shows more imagination than the original combatants themselves displayed. And the depiction of the daily disputes that make up the zany world of Scriblerus often provides a dramatic example of Shaftesbury's dictum that "Great efforts of anger to little purpose, serve for pleasantry and farce."[22]

This attitude toward controversy complicates the response to the debate over identity, as does the Scriblerians' approach to speculative philosophy in general and scholasticism in particular.[23] When the Scriblerians playfully affirm that "the Innate Desire of the knowledge of Metaphysics was the cause of the Fall of Adam," they are expressing a prevalent attitude in that age toward the scholastics and their systems. This irreverence for the jargon of the schoolmen—for what one seventeenth-century writer called the "vain glory of *Syllogizing Sophistry*"—is apparent throughout *The Memoirs* and is consistent with the comments elsewhere by various members of the group. Pope's disdain for the "mighty Scholiast" is well attested by the hordes of "Aristotle's friends" who rumble through *The Dunciad* and gather, in Book 4, at the foot of Dullness herself:

> Prompt at the call, around the Goddess roll
> Broad hats, and hoods, and caps, a sable shoal:
> Thick and more thick the black blockade extends,
> A hundred head of Aristotle's friends.
>
> . . . .
>
> Each staunch Polemic, stubborn as a rock,
> Each fierce Logician, still expelling Locke,
> Came whip and spur, and dash'd thro' thin and thick
> On German Crouzaz, and Dutch Burgersdyck.[24]

Swift's dislike of scholastic thought, indeed of abstruse philosophy of any sort, is more notorious. As Swift informs us

in "The Dean's Reasons For not Building at Drapier's Hill,"
he is

> Sunk over head and ears in matter,
> Nor can of metaphysics smatter.
>
> . . . .
>
> And think all notions too abstracted
> Are like the ravings of a crackt head.[25]

In *A Tale of a Tub*, we recall, the scholastic brother's influence
stems partly from a mastery of Aristotle's corpus, especially
that "wonderful Piece *de Interpretatione*, which has the Faculty
of teaching its Readers to find out a Meaning in every Thing
but itself."[26] Swift, of course, like his fellow Scriblerians Parnell and Arbuthnot, had good reason for an animus toward
the abstracted notions of scholasticism in particular, for they
had all been (in Swift's case, painfully) trained in that very
system.[27] Judging from the fun they have with "Aristotle's
friends" in *The Memoirs*, all the Scriblerians, one suspects,
would have heartily agreed with Joseph Glanvill's definition
of "A *Schoolman*" as "the Ghost of the *Stagirite*, in a Body of
condensed Air."[28]

If we judge solely by such statements and read the Scriblerians' parody of scholastic terminology accordingly, there
should be no problem of tone here when we come to *The
Memoirs*: their attitude toward scholastic thought and language would, expectedly, be uniformly hostile. But the case is
not that simple. It is complicated by the fact that much of the
same language parodied in the work—the word *substance*, for
example—still carried religious and ontological significance.
This accounts for a certain ambivalence of tone that perhaps
reflects the Scriblerians' position in a transitional age, when
one metaphysics was slowly being discarded and no other had
yet risen to take its place.[29] Locke and Berkeley wrestled with
the same problem. In his exchange with Stillingfleet, Locke

repeatedly criticized the bishop's obscure scholastic terms, exclaiming at one point: "I do not find any one that understands them better... than I my self; which indeed is none at all."[30] And in the *Essay*, Locke's critique of the schoolman's "curious and unexplicable Web of perplexed Words" is devastating (3.10.6–12). Yet, despite such attacks, Locke himself is very careful to use the same "perplexed Words" when they carry religious significance.[31] As James Gibson noted some years ago, Locke's theory of personal identity, for example,

> is definitely set over against the current dogmatic [i.e., scholastic] view, which regarded identity of self as consisting in an identity of spiritual substance.... It must be observed, however, that even in this, the maturest product of his criticism, Locke does not succeed in entirely freeing himself from the old way of looking at things. Questions about the identity of an underlying spiritual substance are banished from the realm of our knowledge, but they are not declared to be intrinsically unintelligible. Locke still firmly believes that there is an unknown substrate to the mental life of the individual.[32]

Berkeley shows a similar reticence in confronting the old ontology. In his *Principles of Human Knowledge* he destroys the old scholastic doctrine of material substance; yet Berkeley refuses there and elsewhere to do what Hume (who had no such scruples) later did: to apply the same critique to spiritual substance. Though Berkeley was no great friend of scholasticism, he was wary of any attempt to tamper with the old theological concept of the substantial self, and, as we have seen, he vigorously defended it throughout his career as both a philosopher and a churchman.[33]

Like Berkeley, the Scriblerians were, in their own ways, reasonably religious. This may be a factor that tempers their response to the old scholastic vision. One pole of their attitude is suggested in the hostile responses quoted above; another in Swift's *Remarks* on Tindal's *Rights of the Christian Church*. At one point in the *Rights*, Tindal had called on Locke's authority to attack the *"miserable Gibberish of the Schools"* ostensibly, the same target as that of much of *The Memoirs*. But Swift's reaction to Tindal's attack on scholasticism is seemingly different from anything in *The Memoirs*:

> We have exploded Schoolmen as much as he, and in some People's Opinion too much, since the Liberty of embracing any Opinion is allowed. They following *Aristotle*, who is doubtless the greatest Master of Arguing in the World: But it hath been a Fashion of late Years to explode *Aristotle*, and therefore this Man hath fallen into it like others, for that Reason, without understanding him. *Aristotle's* Poetry, Rhetorick, and Politicks are admirable, and therefore it is likely, so are his Logicks.[34]

W. B. Carnochan has cited this passage, along with another —a humorous attack on Tindal's use of the "refined Way of Speaking...introduced by Mr. *Locke*"[35]—to argue, rightly I believe, against Rosalie Colie's claim that Swift wholly supported Locke in the controversy with Stillingfleet. Though Swift is "properly" ranked, says Carnochan, "with the opponents of scholasticism, it is not quite so clear-cut as that."[36] I would add that, like Berkeley, Swift is aware that one could not dispose of all the language of scholasticism without at the same time destroying Christian tenets couched in that very language. This is precisely what Tindal is doing and what Swift is here attacking.

Swift's position in the *Remarks*, taken with the individual Scriblerian gibes at "Aristotle's friends," helps get at the ambivalent tone we find in *The Memoirs*: on the one hand, a critical and comic disdain for scholasticism, and on the other —present, though often not as pronounced—a lingering awareness of some deeper religious and ontological meanings buried in the same system. A similar ambivalence informs their response, not simply to the old ontology, but also to the more current debate over identity and consciousness. In a Menippean fashion, Pope and his friends comically and characteristically attack the abstruse arguments, metaphysical gymnastics, and supreme duncery involved in such a dispute. Yet, as their parodic handling of the Lockean controversy suggests, they are also concerned with the theological and ethical questions that controversy raised. This is perhaps what Dugald Stewart meant many years ago when, echoing Berkeley's praise of Arbuthnot as a "great philosopher," he said that "an attentive and intelligent reader" of *The Memoirs* "will trace, amid all [the] pleasantry, a metaphysical depth and soundness."[37]

6

"A Master-piece" for
"None but a Philosopher"

Puzzles of Identity in
The Memoirs of Scriblerus

When he was told, a *substance* was that which was *subject*
to accidents; then Soldiers (quoth Crambe) are the most
substantial people in the world.
The Scriblerus Club

Since *The Memoirs* parody pedantic scholarship of all sorts, it
is easy to step into the snare the Scriblerians have set for future
pedants and write a parody of a parody. With this risk in
mind, let us now look specifically at those sections that address the current discussion of identity and consciousness:
chapter 7, "Rhetoric, Logic, and Metaphysics," which tracks
the progress of Martinus Scriblerus's education and picks up
the critique of the substantial self; chapter 12, the Scriblerians' version of the Clarke-Collins dispute, which continues
the play on substance and also comments on the new criterion
of consciousness; and chapters 14 and 15, the Double Mistress
episode, which engages the third theme of the debate, the
puzzles of identity.

Of these themes, the third is perhaps most important to *The
Memoirs*. We earlier looked at some letters in *The British Apollo*
about a pair of Siamese twins. The author of those letters may
have been John Arbuthnot;[1] a similar puzzle provides a basis
for the strange case of the Double Mistress. Martinus himself

falls passionately in love with and marries one of two such twins, which leads to charges of polygamy, incest, rape, and a painstaking series of court trials to determine her/their identity/ies. At one point in *The Memoirs*, we learn that the twins are truly "a Master-piece...for none but a Philosopher" (p. 149). This statement describes not only the case of the curious twins but also the Scriblerians' own exploration of the problem of personal identity.

What Dugald Stewart saw as a mixture of pleasantry and metaphysical depth is evident throughout the Scriblerians' consideration of identity and consciousness, especially their commentary on the substantial self. In chapter 7, where Martinus gets a scholastic education (of sorts), Crambe tells Cornelius Scriblerus

> that All men were not *singular*; that Individuality could hardly be praedicated of any man, for it was commonly said that a man *is* not the same he *was*, that madmen are *beside themselves*, and drunken men *come to themselves*; which shews, that few men have that most valuable logical endowment, Individuality. Cornelius told Martin that a shoulder of mutton was an individual, which Crambe denied, for he had seen it cut into commons: That's true (quoth the Tutor) but you never saw it cut into shoulders of mutton: If it could (quoth Crambe) it would be the most lovely individual of the University.
>
> (p. 119)

On its own, the beginning of this passage is a humorous spoof of Locke's suggestion that the "same Man" could "at different times make different Persons...explained by our way of speaking in *English*," when we say such an one *is "not himself*," or "*besides himself*" (*Essay* 2.27.20). This madman/sober man parody is important, for, along with the ludicrous squabble over the individuality of a shoulder of mutton, the parody establishes the context of Locke's theory and the problem of identity for the series of plays on the substantial self that ensue. In the latter part of the passage, Cornelius's point is that we do not get shoulders of mutton being "beside themselves" like Lockean persons, or replicating themselves as shoulders. If so, Crambe concludes, this individual would be the hungry scholar's delight.

Immediately after this dispute, and the reference to Locke's theory, the following exchange occurs:

> When he was told, a *substance* was that which was *subject to accidents*; then Soldiers (quoth Crambe) are the most substantial people in the world. Neither would he allow it to be a good definition of *accident*, that it could be *present or absent without the destruction of the subject*; since there are a great many accidents that destroy the subject, as burning does a house, and death a man.
>
> (p. 119)

The humor here arises from Crambe's taking the old ontological concept of substance and reversing it. Crambe's account makes substance not, as the definition intends, the subject *of* accidents, but subject *to* accidents, literal accidents. And since soldiers are the most subject to accidents, they are, on his line of thinking, "the most substantial people in the world."

The Scriblerians do not stop here. We may recall that writers in the debate (including Berkeley) continually stress that immaterial substance is indivisible, subsisting, and incapable of being destroyed by the various modes or accidents of which it is the subject. The Scriblerians are parodically working out the possibility—a possibility Locke faced in the *Essay* and one that critics felt his own theory engendered— that substance itself is capable of being destroyed. Thus, to Crambe's contention that "there are a great many accidents that destroy the subject, as burning does a house, and death a man," Cornelius replies "that there was a *natural death*, and *a logical death*; that though a man after his natural death was not capable of the least parish-office, yet he might still keep his Stall amongst the logical praedicaments" (p. 119). Cornelius argues against the possibility that the subject or substance is capable of being destroyed and for the belief that "after his natural death" a man will "still keep his Stall amongst the logical praedicaments": that is, logically—and theologically —the man will continue to persist as a permanent, indestructible substance. In his own singularly literal and ludicrous manner, Cornelius here defends the substantial self. Amid the obvious satire and *ludus* that enliven this exchange, the Scriblerians touch on key issues surrounding the current critique of identity-of-substance. That this same sequence begins with Locke's theory is, one suspects, no accident.

Throughout chapter 7, the plays on the substantial self continue, as when Crambe later argues that his clothes are "more a substance than he was; for his cloaths could better subsist without him, than he without his cloaths" (p. 120). Along with this pleasantry there is simultaneously a suggestion of the possible consequence for identity should that ontological concept be lost. Perhaps nowhere in chapter 7 are both levels more apparent than near its conclusion, when the narrator comments.

> This brings into my mind a Project to banish Metaphysicks out of Spain, which it was suppos'd might be effectuated by this method: That nobody should use any Compound or Decompound of the Substantial Verbs but as they are read in the common conjugations; for every body will allow, that if you debar a Metaphysician from *ens, essentia, entitas, subsistentia*, &c. there is an end of him.
>
> (p. 124)

John Kersey's *Dictionarium* (1708) provides two basic meanings for *subsistence*, the word played on here in "*subsistentia*" and in the passage that follows. Kersey's first definition is "Being, Continuance"; his second, "Food, Livelihood."[2] The Scriblerians employ both connotations in their "Project to banish metaphysicks out of Spain." On the one hand, if you deprive a metaphysician of crabbed "Substantial" words such as *subsistentia*, you deprive him of his "Livelihood" and there is an "end of him." On the other, if you deprive him of his *subsistentia*, there is a literal "*end* of him." He will no longer have "Being" and "Continuance."

A similar play on the old ontological terminology, again with double overtones, continues in the next paragraph, the last in the chapter:

> Crambe regretted extremely, that *Substantial Forms*, a race of harmless beings which had lasted for many years, and afforded a comfortable subsistance to many poor Philosophers, should be now hunted down like so many Wolves, without the possibility of a retreat.... He thought there should be a retreat for poor *substantial Forms*, amongst the Gentlemen-ushers at court; and that there were indeed *substantial forms*, such as *forms of Prayer*, and *forms of Government*, without which, the things themselves could never long subsist.
>
> (p. 124)

With satiric force, the Scriblerians pursue their attack on scholasticism, in this case the cherished "*Substantial Forms*" of Aristotle's friends. The parody of this metaphysics reflects again, however, ontological ramifications of the loss of that vision. In the opening sentence, "subsistance" continues to carry its double sense of both "Livelihood" and "Continuance" of "Being." Thus, the "Substantial Forms"—themselves "*beings* which had *lasted* for many years"—had afforded the philosophers a comfortable "Livelihood" at the same time the "Forms" had enabled them to subsist through time as continuous beings.

Such wordplay tends to balance, and to complicate,

Crambe's mock lament over the hunting down of the substantial vision. On the one hand, the Scriblerians themselves,
like Locke and Berkeley before them, are gladly participating
in the same hunt. On the other, as the various plays on the old
ontology suggest, the Scriblerians are sensitive to the ontological and ethical implications of destroying that vision altogether. Though this same ambivalence appears in their
treatment of the Clarke-Collins controversy in chapter 12, it
tends at times to break down, particularly at one point helpful to our understanding of Crambe's comical lament. Here
the fictionalized Collins argues against the belief that "Punishments cannot be just that are not inflicted upon the same
individual, which cannot subsist without the notion of a spiritual substance"; and he delights in replacing this vision of
the personality with his own, "a flux body" (p. 140). At
such points, the Scriblerians' sympathies appear to be with
a substantialist like Samuel Clarke, and not with Anthony
Collins. And despite the Scriblerians' disdain for scholasticism and its forms, they would seemingly agree with Clarke,
Lee, or Stillingfleet and say of "Individuality" what Crambe
says of "forms of Prayer": without an underlying spiritual
substance, the person "could never long *subsist*."

Chapter 12, "How Martinus endeavoured to find out the
Seat of the Soul," continues the play on the dismissal of substance and adds a critique of Locke's new criterion of consciousness. Both themes emerge in a letter to Martinus from
the "Secretary" of the "Society of Free-thinkers," a fictional
version of Anthony Collins's debate with Samuel Clarke.[3]

The chapter begins with Martinus's attempts, all unsuccessful, to locate empirically the seat of the soul. "Sometimes
he was of [the] opinion," the Scriblerians tell us,

> that it lodg'd in the Brain, sometimes in the Stomach, and
> sometimes in the Heart. Afterwards he thought it absurd to

confine that sovereign Lady to one apartment, which made
him infer that she shifted it according to the several functions
of life: The Brain was her Study, the Heart her State-room,
and the Stomach her Kitchen. But as he saw several offices of
life went on at the same time, he was forc'd to give up this
Hypothesis also.

(p. 137)

Martinus's search seems to be endless, before he arrives at
what appears at least for now to be *the* answer: the *"Glandula
Pinealis."* (Later, in the Double Mistress episode, he will
arrive at still another answer to the question of the seat of the
soul, what he there calls "the *constituent Principle* and *Essence* of
Individuality" [p. 157].) Here the chief satire is directed at attempts such as Descartes's to place the soul in one particular
part of the body. But the sequence also sheds light on the
letter from the "Secretary" of the "Society of Free-thinkers"
that follows. At the same time that it attacks Descartes, it
humorously points to difficulties the epistemical turn had
created in finding that "sovereign Lady": in Locke's case, the
near-impossibility of perceiving, on his principles, that "one
individual immaterial Substance" (*Essay* 2.27.25). In their
debate, Stillingfleet told Locke that questioning our ability to
find that substance had put its being into doubt.[4] Years later,
Andrew Baxter would argue that Locke had also made it possible for others such as Collins to dispense with the term—and
the substantial self—altogether. In his *Enquiry into the Nature
of the Human Soul* (ca. 1733) Baxter tells us that "Mr. *Locke*
allows that the internal, unknown constitution of things is
something; since their discoverable qualities are owned to de-
pend on this.... This is taken notice of because sceptical men
begin to suppose they have Mr. *Locke's* authority for insinu-
ating that the unknown constitution of things is in itself nothing; and that *substance*...is but an empty sound."[5] The Scriblerians play with this same implication in their immediate

movement from Martinus's search to the Secretary's letter, as the difficulties in finding the seat of the soul lead to the question of its existence.

Thus, the Secretary begins his letter by admonishing Martinus for wasting his genius

> in looking after that Theological Non-entity commonly call'd the *Soul*: Since after all your enquiries, it will appear you have lost your labour in seeking the Residence of such a Chimera, that never had being but in the brains of some dreaming Philosophers. Is it not *demonstration* to a person of your Sense, that, since *you cannot find it*, there is *no such thing*? In order to set so hopeful a Genius right in this matter, we have sent you an answer to the ill-grounded Sophisms of those crack-brain'd fellows.
>
> (p. 138)

With this opening, the Scriblerians put the Secretary's ensuing version of the Clarke-Collins controversy squarely within the framework of proving the nonexistence of the substantial soul. This is the occasion of the Secretary's letter, and its central thesis. In his letter, the discarding of the underlying substance or subject, parodied earlier in the Crambe-Cornelius exchange, is here completed. As the Secretary takes up the historical Clarke's main points—"the ill-grounded Sophisms of those crack-brain'd fellows"—and triumphantly refutes them, the seat of consciousness, the substantial self, is eradicated. And with the view of selfhood the Secretary offers in its place, the abiding self becomes an imaginary construct.

The first of the "Sophisms" the Secretary answers is the contention "that *Self-consciousness* cannot inhere in any system of Matter, because all matter is made up of several distinct beings, which never can make up one individual thinking being" (p. 138). This, in broad outline, is the historical Clarke's central argument that "*Self-consciousness*" is an undivided, continuous activity of an underlying subject, that the soul always thinks; and, conversely, that matter, being divisible, could never unite diverse acts into those of "one individual thinking being."[6] In imaginatively recreating the historical Collins's reply—that thought is a divisible mode and that consciousness, not inherent in any one particle of matter, could result from the combined operation of the whole[7]—the Scriblerians take this position to an extreme conclusion. Clarke's argument, the Secretary tells Scriblerus,

> is easily answer'd by a familiar instance: In every *Jack* there is a *meat-roasting* Quality, which neither resides in the Fly, nor in the Weight, nor in any particular wheel of the Jack, but is the result of the whole composition: So in an Animal, the Self-consciousness is not a real quality inherent in one Being (any more than meat-roasting in a Jack) but the result of several modes or qualities in the same subject.... And as the general Quality of meat-roasting...does not inhere in any one part of the Jack; so neither does Consciousness, with its several modes of sensation, intellection, volition, &c. inhere in any one, but is the result from the mechanical composition of the whole Animal.
>
> (pp. 138–39)

The Secretary's "familiar instance" is, of course, ludicrous, and the Scriblerians here are certainly poking fun at the entire debate. But the point is also important. There is just no basis, the Secretary tells Martinus, for the belief in an underlying subject or substance, or the conviction that consciousness must center in "one Being" in order to "make up one individual thinking" person. Consciousness can exist *without* a subject, activity *without* a self, just as the "quality" of meat-roasting does not inhere in "any one part" of the jack but is a result of "the mechanical composition" of the entire machine. No matter how comically expressed, what this position does to the substantial self is to destroy it. This is what the Scriblerians suggest in their fictionalization of Collins's position here and in sections of the letter that follow.

The Secretary next turns to the charge that if consciousness were not a "fixt" individual quality of one being but a "fleeting" mode of matter in the brain, "individual Personality" would be (as the historical Clarke argued) impossible.[8] This charge and the response to it are both deftly handled by the Scriblerians:

> The Parts (say they) of an animal body are perpetually chang'd, and the fluids, which seem to be subject of consciousness, are in a perpetual circulation; so that the same individual particles do not remain in the Brain; from whence it will follow, that the idea of Individual Consciousness must be constantly translated from one particle of matter to another, whereby the particle A, for example, must not only be conscious, but conscious that it is the same being with the particle B that went before.
>
> We answer, this is only a fallacy of the imagination, and is to be understood in no other sense than that maxim of the English Law, that the *King never dies*. This power of thinking, self-moving, and governing the whole Machine, is communicated from every Particle to its immediate Successor; who, as soon as he is gone, immediately takes upon him the Government, which still preserves the Unity of the whole System.
>
> (pp. 139–40)

In the Secretary's view, the power of "self-moving" does not reside in an unchanging, underlying substance; rather, this power passes from one particle of matter in the brain to its "immediate Successor" who, after "he is *gone*," succeeds to yet another. The implication here for any permanent identity is obvious: I am not one fixed "individual thinking being" but a succession of fleeting beings. It is interesting that here and elsewhere, while playing with Collins's arguments, the Scriblerians seem to anticipate Hume by nearly thirty years. For example, the above comparison of the mental life to a series of successors who maintain one government appears nowhere in Collins; but it can be found in Hume's chapter on

"Personal Identity." After asserting that one "thought chaces another, and draws after it a third, by which it is expell'd in its turn," Hume comments, "In this respect, I cannot compare the soul more properly to any thing than to a republic or commonwealth, in which the several members are united by the reciprocal ties of government and subordination, and give rise to other persons, who propagate the same republic in the incessant changes of its parts."[9]

In any case, with the Secretary's early answers, the Scriblerians parodically work out an implication Locke's critics saw in making personal identity distinct from underlying substance and locating that identity instead in consciousness: a materialistic view of the self, which insures that there will, in one contemporary's words, "be Persons enough to people the world, in every single Body, without going to the Moon or the rest of the Planets for Inhabitants."[10] Despite the Secretary's comic use of the old maxim, "the *King never dies*," the same being on his scheme could (in his own words) persist largely as "a fallacy of the imagination."

Against Clarke's repeated charges that he had made personal identity an "imaginary Denomination," Collins, we recall, resorted in his last pamphlet to "Mr. *Locke's* Chapter of *Identity* and *Diversity*." And in presenting his position on the "Question of Identity," Collins seemed to substantiate many of Clarke's charges. Though Collins tried to argue on Locke's principles that "Memory extending to past Actions" would affirm personal identity, his argument tended to suggest that "we are not conscious, that we continue a Moment the same individual numerical Being."[11]

In the Scriblerian version, the Secretary also relies on Locke's criterion of consciousness. The questions of whether consciousness needs a subject and whether the "same being" could persist through a change of substance lead here to a comic consideration of Locke's theory and its ethical and ontological implications. Like his historical counterpart, the Scriblerians' Secretary takes Locke's criterion to a conclusion that makes "the Individuality of Man...alter every Moment."[12] "They make a great noise," the Secretary tells Martinus, "about this Individuality: how a man is conscious to himself that he is the same Individual he was twenty years ago; not-withstanding the flux state of the Particles of matter that compose his body." This, the Secretary continues, can be answered by yet another "familiar instance":

> Sir John Cutler had a pair of black worsted stockings, which his maid darn'd so often with silk, that they became at last a pair of silk stockings. Now supposing those stockings of Sir John's endued with some degree of Consciousness at every particular darning, they would have been sensible, that they were the same individual pair of stockings both before and after the darning; and this sensation would have continued in them through all the succession of darnings; and yet after the last of all, there was not perhaps one thread left of the first pair of stockings, but they were grown to be silk stockings, as was said before.
>
> (p. 140)

The familiar example by which the Secretary demonstrates his principle of identity-in-consciousness is again ludicrous, but with a point. By means of their "Consciousness" the stockings would be sensible "after" the darning that they were the "same individual" stockings as "before." But, as the rest of the passage suggests, they would be mistaken. This is a brilliant burlesque of Collins's use of Locke's theory, in this case, the contention that "as far as this consciousness can be extended backwards to any past Action or Thought, so far reaches the Identity of that *Person*" (*Essay*, 2.27.9). In choosing a physical object to demonstrate the Secretary's point, the Scriblerians are of course satirizing Collins's materialism. But they are also working out, in parodic terms, a main ontological implication early critics saw in the new view of identity-in-consciousness: the conclusion of a Collins, which argues the transience of the self.

After a further argument, in which the Secretary continues to refute the need for "some individual self-moving ... principle," the Scriblerians turn to the ethical ramifications of Collins's position. In his last two pamphlets, we recall, Clarke told Collins that by locating identity in such a fluid medium and by making it feasible "that *One Man* may possibly be *two Persons*" he had destroyed the principle "upon which ... the Justice of Reward and Punishment" in this world "manifestly depends." Collins's approach had also made "a future State of Rewards and Punishments not only *Improbable*, but *Impossible*; seeing that it infers ... an absolute *Impossibility* of a *Resurrection of the same Person*." [13]

The Scriblerians' Secretary has an easy answer to such accusations. He tells Martinus that it is "objected, that Punishments cannot be just that are not inflicted upon the same individual, which cannot subsist without the notion of a spiritual substance. We reply, that this is no greater difficulty to conceive, than that a Corporation, which is likewise a flux body, may be punished for the faults, and liable to the debts, of their Predecessors" (p. 140). As was suggested in the Secretary's dismissal of the underlying "spiritual substance" and his positing instead a radical concept of the self-in-consciousness, the implication developed here is clear: the dissolution not only of that "one individual thinking being" but also of the ethical liability that "manifestly depends" on the person remaining the same. Thus, in the humor that pervades the letter from the Secretary to Martinus, the Scriblerians point to ramifications contemporaries saw in Collins's reading of Locke.

These implications are picked up in the wordplay in the chapter's conclusion. The first occurs at the close of the Secretary's letter, and in a playful manner that recalls the Scriblerians' earlier games with the old ontology. "We wait with the utmost impatience for the honour of having you a Member of our Society," the Secretary tells Martinus, "and beg leave to *assure you that we are*, &c." In light of the ontological ramifications of the Secretary's approach, there would seem to be, the Scriblerians suggest, little such lasting assurance. The ethical implication suggests itself in the chapter's concluding sentence, in which Crambe advises Martinus "by no means to enter into their Society, unless they would give him sufficient security, to bear him *harmless* from any thing that might happen after this present life" (p. 142, my italics). On the Secretary of the Society's interpretation of the self-inconsciousness, Martinus would indeed be safe from any consequences of his present actions. For, as the Secretary's entire letter to him humorously suggests, Martinus would by no means be the same, accountable person "after this present life" or in any two moments of this one.

Leslie Fiedler tells a story about Rosa and Josepha, who had a smash vaudeville act. One person who knew these Siamese twins, Edward Malone, recounted how

> when they had begun "to hit the big time" in 1921, Josepha announced that she was (a) pregnant and (b) still a virgin: a "misconception" which tickled the reporters of the period. At that point, however, a carpenter called Franzel embarrassed them both (Rosa having sworn that her sister was telling the truth) by claiming to be the expectant father and offering to marry Josepha. But when after much shilly-shallying, the twins acknowledged that he might after all have been responsible, no minister or judge would perform the ceremony, lest he compound their previous "moral turpitude."[14]

In *The Memoirs*, the Scriblerians invent a parallel situation of similar complexity. Here, too, a third theme of the debate, the puzzles of identity, comes into prominence.

In a passage parodied earlier in *The Memoirs*, Locke had maintained that it was indeed possible, on his grounds, for the "same Man" to be "different Persons." As we have seen, this puzzling conclusion and its ethical consequences bothered some contemporaries. If it were possible for the "same Man" to be "beside himself," how could that man, they argued, be fairly judged? In the Scriblerians' story of the Double Mistress, we have this Lockean puzzle literalized, an actual case of two persons *beside themselves* in the same body: a set of beautiful Siamese twins. The Scriblerians take the popular case of the Hungarian twins, as well as the puzzle questions they provoked in *The British Apollo*, and develop these materials into a burlesque romance between Martinus and the girls, a tale that reveals "as extraordinary a Conjunction of Passions as of Persons" (p. 152). In exploiting the comic possibilities latent in such materials, they also take Locke's question of "sameness" to perplexing heights, before Martinus answers it in depth. During a trial scene in chapter 15—which plays with the puzzling ramifications of that question—Martinus arrives at his own criterion of personal identity, one which definitively locates the "*Essence* of *Individuality*."

In chapter 14 the Scriblerians tell the passionate tale of Martinus's attachment to the "two Bohemian Sisters," Lindamira and Indamora, "whose common Parts of Generation, had so closely allied them, that Nature seem'd here to have conspired with Fortune, that their lives should run in an eternal Parallel." While visiting a freak show, replete with a tiny Black Prince, a "glaring Cat-a-mountain" and a "Man-mimicking Manteger," Martinus first sets eyes upon Lindamira and Indamora, "the most beautiful Curiosity of Nature." In Martinus, the Scriblerians comment, both the "Fire of Youth" and the "unquenchable Curiosity of a Philosopher" are immediately "pitch'd upon the same object" (p. 146). Yet, it is precisely the question of whether Lindamira-Indamora is, in fact, the "same object" that is comically posed in the plot complications and the plays on "sameness," singleness, and doubleness that follow. As Martinus begins to visit the twins daily, Randal, the "monster-master," becomes suspicious of the lover's intentions. It "was no small cause of wonder to Mr. Randal," we are told, "that this Gentleman should come every day to behold the *same* show. He, no less covetous than the Guardian of *a* rich *Heiress*, entertain'd a suspicion that Martin had a design of stealing *the Ladies*" (p. 148, my italics). The play here is in the movement from singular to plural. Is Lindamira-Indamora an "Heiress" or "the Ladies"? This puzzling play on singleness and doubleness recurs throughout the chapter, most notably in Martinus's later struggle with one of Randal's monsters. Tricked by Randal into a midnight assignation with the lady/ies, Martin meets instead the fierce Cat-a-mountain. The heroic battle that erupts wakes the house and creates this scene:

> The apartment of the Bohemian Beauties being the adjoining Room, they were the first that enter'd with a light to his assistance. Martin all bloody as he was, a most fierce Cat-a-mountain hanging at his chin... at the sight of Lindamira forgot his distress. Ah, my Love! (he cried) how like is thy fate to that of Thisbe! who staying but a moment too late, found, as she thought, her miserable Lover torn in pieces by a Savage beast! The affrighted Damsels shriek'd aloud; Mr. Randal with all his Retinue rush'd into the room; and now every hand conspired to free his under-jaw from the sharp teeth of the enraged Monster. But the Lady, whose heart melted at the piteous Spectacle, was so zealous in this office of Humanity, that the Cat-a-mountain... leap'd furiously on her, and wounded three of her hands and her two noses, to such a barbarous degree, that she was not fit to be shown publickly for the space of three weeks.

(p. 150)

We here move from plural ("the Beauties") to singular (Martinus's "Ah, my Love!") to plural ("affrighted Damsels") back to singular ("the Lady") and finally to a grotesque mixture of both: the Cat-a-mountain wounds "*her* two noses." The Scriblerians again raise this question: Is Lindamira-Indamora singular or plural, one or two persons?

This puzzling question is further enhanced by complications in plot. Martinus's affections, it seems, are clearly set on Lindamira, which poses a love problem for Indamora. For "Fate had so ordain'd, that Martin was not more enamoured on Lindamira, than Indamora was on Martin. She, jealous that her Sister had the greatest share in this conquest, resented that an equal application had not been made to herself." What a predicament, the narrator comments, for her to be "depriv'd the universal Relief of a *Soliloquy*" (p. 151). Yet, Indamora, in an apostrophe, arrives at her own singular reconciliation of this problem of love:

> Wretched Indamora! if Lindamira must never more see Martin, Martin shall never again bless the eyes of Indamora. Yet why do I say wretched, since my Rival can never possess my Lover without me? The pangs that others feel in Absence, from the thought of those Joys that bless their Rivals, can never sting thy bosom; nor can they mortify thee by making thee a Witness, without giving thee at the same time a share, of their Endearments.
>
> (pp. 151–52)

The three lovers are thus reconciled. After a harrowing escape from Randal's house—during which the twins become caught in an upper window and barely miss rape by the "Man-mimicking Manteger"—Martinus and his "double Lucrece" are happily wedded at the chapter's conclusion.

Chapter 15 treats the tragic events that conspire to "make these three lovers unhappy." The puzzling question of the twins' identity, developed in the previous chapter, is complicated further as the girls' identity becomes the subject of a *"never to be parallel'd* Process *at* Law" (p. 154). Here, too, Martinus arrives at his own distinctive answer to the problem of personal identity.

Angered at Martinus's elopement, Randal seizes the girls by court order and plots litigious revenge against the groom. The showmaster resolves to commence a suit against Martinus for *"Bigamy* and *Incest."* To help his position he forces Indamora into a clandestine marriage to the Black Prince, which is accomplished in Lindamira's sleep. With these further complications, Martinus turns plaintiff. And the ensuing trial scenes take the puzzles of identity to a comic reductio ad absurdum. Martinus's lawyer, Dr. Penny-Feather, accuses the Black Prince of a host of improprieties in presuming "to marry this Our Wife." In marrying the twins, Penny-Feather argues, the Black Prince has maintained "no less an absurdity than this, that *One* is *Two*; and that Lindamira-Indamora, the individual wife of the Plaintiff, is not *one*, but *two Persons"* (p. 156). Following this statement, Penny-Feather wages an elaborate defense of Martinus's position. The lawyer's central argument is that "Lindamira-Indamora, now our lawful wife, makes but one individual Person" (p. 157).

In demonstrating this point, Penny-Feather tells the court, it will be necessary "to determine the *constituent Principle* and *Essence* of *Individuality."* He then presents, in Scriblerian mock logic, the orthodox theological concept of the self, before subverting it. In respect to persons, Penny-Feather argues, we usually take the criterion of *"Individuality"* to be "one simple identical soul, in one simple identical body." But the "individuality, sameness, or identity of [that] body, is not determin'd (as some vainly imagine) by one head, and a certain number of arms, legs, and other members; but in one simple, single...member of Generation." Thus, ancient monsters like Geryon or Briareus were never considered "more than

one Person" because each had only "one Member of Generation" which made him "one single person" (p. 157).

This is Martinus Scriblerus's singular contribution to the
current discussion of personal identity. And his lawyer proceeds to apply this criterion not simply to the "charming
Monsters" but to the rest of humankind. In his argument,
the organ of generation becomes the locus of the entire personality. As "there is but one Member of Generation,"
Penny-Feather states,

> there is but one body, so there can be but one Soul; because
> the said organ of Generation is the Seat of the Soul; and con-
> sequently, where there is but one such Organ, there can be
> but one Soul. Let me here say ... that no Philosopher, either
> of the past or present age, hath taken more pains to discover
> where the Soul keeps her residence, than the Plaintiff, the
> learned Martinus Scriblerus: And after his most diligent en-
> quiries and experiments, he hath been verily persuaded, that
> the Organ of Generation is the true and only *Seat of the Soul*.
> That this part is seated in the middle, and near the Centre
> of the whole body, is obvious to your Honour's view. From
> thence, like the sun in the Centre of the world, the Soul dis-
> penses her warmth and vital influence.... It is to the Organs
> of Generation that we owe Man himself; there the Soul is em-
> ployed in her works suitable to the Dignity of her Nature, and
> (as we may say) sits brooding over ages yet unborn.
>
> (pp. 157–58)

In demonstrating Martinus's criterion, Penny-Feather introduces irrefutable proofs. He asks, for example, why some
women who are "deaf to the persuasions of the Eloquent" or
"the insinuations of the Crafty" so easily give into "some poor
Logger-head." The answer is simple. Unlike the others, he
makes "immediate application to this *Seat of the Soul*." Penny-
Feather concludes that, on Martinus's criterion, Lindamira-
Indamora has "but *one* Organ of Generation" and is there-

fore "*one individual Person,* in the truest and most proper sense of Individuality." To this contention he adds two points: even if they were "*two* individual Persons," they would "have but one Organ of Generation" and could thus "constitute but one wife"; moreover, if they were two persons, Martinus would still be entitled to both. Why? For in marrying Lindamira, he acquired "*all other Matter inseparably annex'd unto her*" (pp. 158–60). In the lawyer's arguments, the Scriblerians seemingly take this puzzling case to its comic and logical limits.

But the Black Prince's lawyer, Dr. Leather-head, goes even further. In his defense he accuses Martinus of degrading "this Queen, the Rational Soul, to the very lowest and vilest Apartment"; and he argues instead that "personal Individuality did subsist, when there was no such generative Carnality." As to Martinus's second point—that even if they were two persons, with one organ of generation they would still constitute one wife—Leather-head argues: "if there be but one such Organ of Generation, then both the persons of Lindamira and Indamora have an equal property in it; and what is Indamora's property cannot be dispos'd of without her consent." If Martinus had Indamora's consent, the lawyer contends, "he is guilty of *Bigamy*; if not, he is guilty of a *Rape*, or *Incest*, or both" (pp. 161–62). Finally, even on Martinus's grounds they are still two persons; for they do have, the lawyer contends, two distinct organs of generation!

After taking this puzzling case to its perplexing heights, the Scriblerians conclude the trial with an equally wild decision. "Gentlemen," the judge declares,

> I am of opinion that Lindamira and Indamora are distinct persons, and that both the Marriages are good and valid: Therefore I order you, Martinus Scriblerus, Batchelor in Physick, and you, Ebn-Hai-Paw-Waw, Prince of Monomotapa, to cohabit with your wives, and to lie in bed each on the

side of his own wife. I hope, Gentlemen, you will seriously consider, that you are under a stricter Tye than common Brothers-in law; that being, as it were, joint Proprietors of one common Tenement, you will so behave as good fellow lodgers ought to do, and with great modesty each to his respective sister-in-law, abstaining from all farther Familiarities than what Conjugal Duties do naturally oblige you to. Consider also by how small Limits the Duty and the Trespass is divided, lest, while ye discharge the duty of Matrimony, ye heedlesly slide into the sin of Adultery.

(pp. 162–63)

Martinus and the Prince do not, of course, have much opportunity to slide into sin, for the litigation does not end here. This decision leads instead to a baffling series of appeals and judgments that culminate finally in a different decision of a higher court. In a ruling that brings the episode to a close, the court concludes that "two persons could not have a Right to the entire possession of the same thing, at the same time." Both marriages are therefore dissolved, "as proceeding upon a natural, as well as legal Absurdity" (p. 163).

Such a puzzle indeed is a "Master-piece... for none but a Philosopher." By taking a baffling case of two persons in the same body to its logical and comical absurdity, the Scriblerians are again satirizing (among other things) the tedious complexity of much of the current debate. And their presentation seems, at the least, to undercut the entire issue. Yet, as earlier, the Scriblerians also point here to pertinent questions the problem of "sameness" posed. It is no accident, for instance, that their play on the puzzles of identity simultaneously becomes a satire of the legal profession. For personal identity itself is undeniably a legal problem, especially in the light of Locke's theory.[15] Martinus's burlesque criterion for defining personal identity "in its truest and most proper sense" is likewise satiric; yet the Scriblerians' consideration of the question acknowledges, at the same time, the *need* for a criterion. In summing up the group's imaginative response to the current discussion of identity and consciousness, we can return with some justice to Maclean's statement about their "interested antipathy for philosophy" and rephrase it. The Scriblerians' approach to the dispute certainly reveals an antipathy for the subject; but it is, nonetheless, an interested one.

Epilogue

If you ask me by what Artifice a Man is able to perform the
Rational and Discursive Actions of the Phantasy, Intellect,
Memory, &c.? I will answer, that they are done in an
Admirable and Spiritual Manner: But if you demand what the
Manner is, and how produced? I must answer, it is done, I
know not how, by the Power of the Soul: shew me a Soul, and
I will tell you how it works.

Sir Kenelm Digby

"It is an old observation," writes Abraham Tucker in 1763,
"that nothing is more difficult for a Man to know than himself." But this, he argues, was understood in earlier ages as
"the knowledge of a Man's character"; it was never "esteemed difficult to know his own person from that of another.
... Whereas a difficulty has been lately started in ascertaining
what is properly *the Man*, or to what the pronoun *I* ought to
be applied."[1] About the time of Tucker's statement, *Tristram
Shandy* points (more playfully) to similar difficulties: "My
good friend, quoth I—as sure as I am I—and you are you—
And who are you? said he.——Don't puzzle me, said I."[2]

Such comments suggest that identity remained an issue
long after Locke and well into the century. In his 1763 com-
pendium of problems in pneumatology, ethics, and divinity
—a work that serves as an excellent sourcebook for primary
writings in what we would call psychology—Philip Doddridge notes that the "question wherein personal identity
consists" is indeed still "attended with some perplexities";
and this, despite explanations by "persons of great learn-

ing."[3] Perhaps even *because of* such explanations, the Scriblerians might add. In *The Memoirs of Scriblerus*, such explanations become the stuff of comedy. Perplexities build on perplexities. Words generate, not answers, but more words, and we gradually find ourselves in a comedy of higher lunacy. After looking at the Scriblerians' review of the contemporary discussion of identity, it is tempting to wonder how they might have responded to Byron's comment about Coleridge

> Explaining metaphysics to the nation—
> I wish he would explain his Explanation.[4]

It is also tempting to take *The Memoirs* as the Scriblerians' last word on the subject, especially given the papers' relatively late date of publication. This is tempting but probably wrong, for several reasons. Though *The Memoirs* were published in 1741, they had their inception (as we have seen) at a much earlier date. We should also perhaps remember some later work by a younger member of the group, Alexander Pope, who prepared the Scriblerus papers for press. Recent studies have said something about the growing complexity of his consideration of identity, broadly defined.[5] Pointing to Pope's poetry of the 1730s, John Sitter for one has argued that if "Addison's desire was to bring philosophy to the coffee house, Pope's is to take poetry to philosophy, especially to that branch of philosophy now regarded as psychology."[6]

In closing it might help, then, to look briefly at several uses Pope makes of the contemporary discussion of identity and consciousness. Take, for instance, the *Epistle to Cobham* (1734), which addresses at least two themes we have examined: Locke's critique of the substantial self, and his attempt to locate identity instead in consciousness. Georges Poulet has said that it "is the greatness of the eighteenth century to have conceived the prime moment of consciousness as a generative moment ... not only of other moments but also of a self which takes shape by and through the means of these very moments."⁷ As I have tried to suggest, however, this view was not accepted immediately. Pope's *Cobham* in 1734 stands in an interesting historical relation to the movement between the older vision of the self as substantial and the newer vision of the self-in-consciousness; between the earliest, hostile responses to Locke's new criterion of consciousness—say, Stillingfleet's puzzled "How comes *Person* to stand for *this?*" in 1698—and Hume's pronouncement in 1740 that "Most philosophers" now seem "inclin'd to think, that personal identity *arises* from consciousness."⁸ For in this work Pope attempts to reconcile, in his own eclectic manner, the two visions of the self. This attempt at reconciling the two visions accounts, I believe, for a central problem in the poem: that is, the relation between Pope's opening section (1–173), with its emphasis on the transience, fluidity, and inscrutability of the human personality, and his closing section (174–265), which introduces the ruling passion to argue that beneath these fluctuations there is an observable consistency at the core.

Locke recognized that the problem of identity could not be separated from the problem of knowledge. As we noted in Part II, it was in all likelihood the problem of finding the substantial soul that led Locke to search for a new criterion of identity, another way of saying that we are the same persons. In a chapter that provides the analogue for Pope's lines on the "microscopic eye" in *An Essay on Man*,⁹ Locke emphasizes our inability to glimpse empirically (much less know) the substantial self, an entity that remains a "supposed *something*" of which "we have no clear distinct *Idea* at all" (*Essay Concerning Human Understanding* 2.23.37). Elsewhere he remarks that it is "past controversy, that we have in us something that thinks, our very Doubts about what it is, confirm the certainty of its being, though we must content our selves in the Ignorance of what kind of *Being* it is" (4.3.6). In 1697, he would tell Still ingfleet that all we know of this underlying substance is "the obscure, indistinct, vague Idea ... of *something*";[10] and this word, referring to the substantial self, would recur throughout the controversy.

Thirty years later, for example, in the second edition of his *Procedure, Extent, and Limits of the Human Understanding* (1729), Peter Browne would complain that Locke has "confounded the received way of thinking and speaking" about such subjects. Soon afterward, Browne himself nevertheless tells us that "in this Life" we have no clear idea of the soul. For this reason,

> we are naturally led to express it by a *Negative*, and call it an Immaterial Substance; that is, something which hath a *Being* but is not Matter; something that *Is*, but is not any thing we directly know; and for want of any direct and positive Idea of it, we conceive and express it after the best manner we can; saying it is *Something*.[11]

A decade after that, while discussing his own problematic attempts to "catch *myself*," Hume would argue that someone else "may, perhaps, perceive *something* simple and continu'd, which he calls *himself*; tho' [and a big "tho'"] this is] I am certain there is no such principle in me."[12]

Like his contemporaries, Pope connects the problem of identity with the problem of knowledge. At an early point in the *Epistle to Cobham*, subtitled *Of Knowledge and the Characters of Men*, the poet remarks:

> *Something* as dim to our internal view,
> Is thus, perhaps, the cause of most we do.[13]

In positing that our personality does inhere in "something" simple and individual, Pope here, unlike Hume, supports the substantial vision of the self. But like Locke before him, the poet is also aware of the dimness of that "something," of our inability to glimpse that unique core of selfhood and "our Ignorance of what kind of *Being* it is." This problem of knowledge and character—that is, the difficulty of finding an inherent "sameness" in the apparent chaos of individual thought and action—is a central theme of the poem.

In presenting that theme in his opening section (1–173), Pope works out his own poetic version of the self-in-consciousness, which was just beginning in the 1730s to gain some acceptance. Attempting to find language to describe the Lockean self and its implications, writers turned to the image of the river. In its Heraclitean sense, this image had of course long been used to depict the outer flux of the world-in-time. But with Locke's theory and the subsequent controversy over it, the river becomes an apt metaphor for the incessant fluctuations in the *inner* world of consciousness, a world in which successive ideas are always "passing in train, one going, and another coming, without intermission" (*Essay* 2.7.9). Our "consciousness," Thomas Reid writes in his critique of Locke, is "still flowing like the water of a river, or like time itself. The consciousness I have this moment, can no more be the same consciousness I had the last moment, than this moment can be the last moment."[14] Earlier in the century, Berkeley speaks of the "floating ideas" of what he sees as an ever-changing consciousness;[15] and Clarke evokes the same image in cataloguing the ramifications of Collins's Lockean vision. By arguing that consciousness is a "fleeting" activity and that "the person may be the same by a continual Superaddition of the *like Consciousness*," Collins had made "individual Personality" a "mere *external imaginary Denomination*," just as, Clarke adds, "a *River* is called the *same River*, though the Water of it be every Day new."[16] Pope employs the same image in his own evocation of the new vision of the self:

> Our depths who fathoms, or our shallows finds,
> Quick whirls, and shifting eddies, of our minds?

> Life's stream for Observation will not stay,
> It hurries all too fast to mark their way.
> In vain sedate reflections we would make,
> When half our knowledge we must snatch, not take.
>
> (29–34)

Pope here posits the dual nature of experience in consciousness, of the self looking outward on the ever-fleeting stream of human experience and, simultaneously, reflecting on its own operations. And what we observe on both levels, Pope intimates, is a state of incessant change and successive motion, the continual hurrying of "Life's stream" both within and without the self. Any attempt at a "sedate" reflection in this ever-changing human world is "vain," for both the observer and what he observes—be it another or himself—simply will not "stay." The poet's emphasis here is the emphasis of the rest of the opening section: the "Quick whirls, and shifting eddies, of our minds" and the near-impossibility of charting these currents in others, much less in ourselves, with any accuracy. Here, too, Pope develops an attendant implication some critics saw in Locke's theory, that the personality is a transient thing. This seems to be a central motif of Pope's opening, as he repeatedly portrays the puzzling ways the "same man" is, ironically, *not* the same any two moments of his life:

> See the same man, in vigour, in the gout;
> Alone, in company; in place, or out;
> Early at Bus'ness, and at Hazard late;
> Mad at a Fox-chace, wise at a Debate;
> Drunk at a Borough, civil at a Ball,
> Friendly at Hackney, faithless at Whitehall.
>
> (130–35)

Although Pope raises the question of "sameness" prominently, he does not, finally, take the self-in-consciousness to the conclusion of a Collins or a Hume. There is, after all, "something" underlying our experience, even though this substantial self remains ever "dim to our internal view." In his closing section (174–265), Pope still does not admit our ability to find that "something" with any certainty. But he does advance a modified version of the older vision by offering us another way of assuring ourselves that beneath the fluctuations of a seemingly transient self there is an observable permanence at the core. And observing this principle of permanence, which is perhaps most apparent at death, we will have a way of perceiving some real connection between the changes.[17] This principle of permanence—and, perhaps, Pope's direct response to the problem of personal identity—is the ruling passion, a knowable manifestation of that unknowable "something."

Though F. W. Bateson and others have found this doctrine in *Cobham* to be theoretically silly, a young contemporary of Pope's, David Hume, apparently did not. In Book 1 of his *Treatise*, Hume speaks of a "prevailing passion" to which persons are "naturally inclined." Later on in the same book, in his chapter on personal identity, Hume argues that "personal identity" may be considered two ways: as it pertains to the understanding or imagination, "*and* as it regards our passions." Though the passions are not the subject of this chapter, they are the subject of Hume's second book, where he talks at one point about a ruling passion becoming a "settled principle of action" and, at another, about how a "predominant passion swallows up" an inferior one "and converts it [to] itself." And "hence one master Passion in the breast," Pope had written, "Like Aaron's serpent, swallows up the rest."[18] Whether Hume works out the implications of the prevailing passion vis à vis personal identity is unimportant here. Of interest is his willingness, like that of Pope before him, to consider the passions in that context.

Despite Pope's attempt to find a principle of permanence, the *Epistle to Cobham* seems to reflect a larger stress in his poetry of the 1730s on the fluidity of the self and the difficulties of "fixing" it for more than a moment at a time. Melinda Alliker Rabb has noted a related emphasis, in the *Horatian Poems* of the same decade, on "fractured images" of the self.[19] Consider, for instance, the lines to Bolingbroke in *The First Epistle of the First Book of Horace* (1738), where Pope tells his interlocutor and friend:

> You laugh, if Coat and Breeches strangely vary,
> White Gloves, and Linnen worthy Lady Mary!
> But when no Prelate's Lawn with Hair-shirt lin'd,
> Is half so incoherent as my Mind,
> When (each Opinion with the next at strife,
> One ebb and flow of follies all my Life)
> I plant, root up, I build, and then confound,
> Turn round to square, and square again to round.
>
> . . . .
>
> [You] hang your lip, to see a Seam awry!
> Careless how ill I with myself agree;
> Kind to my dress, my figure, not to Me.[20]

The emphasis here is on the lack of coherence Pope senses in himself, on the gaps or (to extend his clothes metaphor) seams in experience. A year later, Hume would notice a similar discontinuity in his experience and point to difficulties of catching "*myself*" from one moment to another or of finding something continued that he could call "*himself*."[21] Both the poet and the philosopher are responding, at least in part, to problems that result from a new way of looking at the self and from the gradual displacement by consciousness of what we used to call our souls.

This is perhaps the most significant development in the discussion of the self from the publication of Locke's "Of Identity and Diversity" in 1694 to Vincent Perronet's defense of

Locke's chapter in 1738.[22] By the end of this period, despite continuing protests by Butler and others, consciousness is coming to be viewed as the criterion of personal identity.

That shift is evident in a variety of contexts. We have watched Hume, for instance, at the beginning of the 1740s, ascribe the new criterion to most philosophers. A decade later, another philosopher would argue that an individual is "the same with himself at different times" because he has "continued Consciousness." "This," we hear in 1752, "is the usual and common Sense of the Word *Person*."[23] (As we discovered, this was not the case before Locke.) In medical and physiological writings at midcentury, there was a corresponding tendency to use *consciousness* as a synonym for *soul* or simply to dispense with the latter term altogether, to the dismay of pious physicians such as Robert Whytt.[24] Among literary authors, we have seen suggestions in Pope that the self-in-consciousness was starting to gain a certain currency. This is more clearly marked in such later writers as Richardson, Sterne, and Boswell.

The last author seems to show how quickly, after so much early resistance, the new criterion caught on. As is often noted, Boswell appears almost intuitively to embrace the self-in-consciousness— a vision that, only a few generations before, had been seen as altering "the whole *Frame* of the... *intellectual* World."[25] Boswell is often commended for his modern sensibility, his confirmation of the belief that "it is this minute-by-minute content of consciousness which constitutes what the individual's personality really is."[26] When we consider his close attention to a daily record of "variations within," themselves almost "too fleeting to be recorded," this seems to be the case.[27]

Yet even Boswell demonstrates that the new view was accepted only gradually. For his journals reveal a problem similar to Pope's in reconciling the newer concept with the older belief, the empirical with the substantial self. The search for an underlying "sameness," for what Boswell calls his "real" or "natural" character, is a central theme of his work. In *The London Journal*, for example, he laments:

> Could I but fix myself in such a character and preserve it uniformly, I should be exceedingly happy. I hope to do so and to attain a constancy and dignity without which I can never be satisfied, as I have these ideas strong and pride myself in thinking that my *natural character* is that of dignity. My friend Temple is very good in consoling me by saying that I may be such a man, and that people will say, "Mr. Boswell is quite altered from the dissipated, inconstant fellow that he was. He is now a reserved, grave sort of a man. But indeed that *was his real character*; and he only deviated into these eccentric paths for a while." [28]

Here the difficulty of finding a permanent self becomes a personal crisis. Boswell's preoccupation with the self-in-consciousness makes his attempt to locate a "real" character —one that "was" there all the time—an even more difficult task. As Locke's critics had argued and a modern critic points out, one problem of identifying the self "with the passing moment is that the moment passes." [29] With Boswell, the problem of persistence remains, and thirteen years later we find him still hoping "that if I keep in constant remembrance the thoughts of my heart and imaginations of my fancy, there will be a sameness produced, and my mind will not have free scope for alteration." [30]

One scholar of the later period has noted that nothing "is more common in eighteenth century literature and philosophy than the search for a 'true self,' a self that is often... regarded both as an individual's 'real' identity and as a principle from which he can derive the greatest moral significance. Yet this essential self," the author adds, "proves very difficult to discover." [31] This seems to be true of Boswell's search for a real self. In his unsuccessful search for "sameness" and his often overpowering sense of his own discontinuity—what Johnson saw as the vacuity of being—Boswell shares with other later eighteenth-century writers what Fredric Bogel has described as a "troubled awareness of the insubstantiality of experience" that "threatened not only the fabric of the external world, but the wholeness and continuity of the self as well." Bogel approaches that crisis largely through R. D. Laing's concepts of "ontological insecurity" and the "divided self." [32] Late eighteenth-century writers would (I suspect) find other ways of talking about it, in terms laid down by Locke. For instance, Edmund Law in *A Defence of Mr. Locke's Opinion concerning Personal Identity* (1769) argues that

> however fluctuating and changeful [Locke's] account may be judged to render personality; how much soever it may fall short of some sublime systems about purely immaterial substances... yet there is no help for these changes in the seat of the personality; since, in the last place, we know of nothing more stable and permanent in our constitution that has the least pretence to settle and support it.[33]

Insubstantiality and change here become facts of life; any search for an abiding self runs into difficulty.

What Boswell called that "real" self—or Edward Young that "Stranger within thee"[34]—Pope and early eighteenth-century writers called that "something." And if we recall that similar difficulties in locating the substantial self were previously parodied in *The Memoirs of Scriblerus*, we can perhaps see the intellectual roots of the later crisis in the early part of the century. This point also suggests itself in another late work, William Cowper's *The Task* (1785). In this poem, Cowper claims:

> I am conscious, and confess,
> Fearless, a soul that does not always think.[35]

A recent study has seen this idea as "embryonic in Cowper's day," these lines as "epochal," and the self-in-consciousness, more generally, as a late eighteenth-century invention.[36] The present work will, I hope, spark a reassessment of such views. Almost ninety years before Cowper wrote those lines, Thomas Burnet told Locke: "I do not understand how the Soul, if she be at any time utterly without Thoughts, what it is that produces the first Thought again, at the end of that unthinking Interval.... What is it then that lights the Candle again, when it is put out?"[37] It is interesting that once the eighteenth century had questioned the presence of a substantial self, Kant and the nineteenth century would find other ways to keep the candle burning, by going beneath the "threshold of consciousness" to discover a noumenal self—or a *sub*conscious one.[38] That, however, is another story. The present one has ended.

Notes

INTRODUCTION

1. Joseph Addison and Richard Steele, *The Spectator*, ed. D. F. Bond, 5 vols. (Oxford: Clarendon Press, 1965), 4:575; and Anthony, Earl of Shaftesbury, *Characteristics of Men, Manners, Opinions, Times*, ed. J. M. Robertson, 2 vols. (1900; reprint ed., Gloucester, Mass.: Peter Smith, 1963), 2:275.

2. Alexander Pope et al., *The Memoirs of the Extraordinary Life, Works, and Discoveries of Martinus Scriblerus*, ed. Charles Kerby-Miller (1950; reprint ed., New York: Russell and Russell, 1966), p. 140. Though *The Memoirs* remained unpublished until 1741, the editor (p. 285) gives 1714 as the date of the composition of the chapter in which this comment appears.

3. George Berkeley, *Alciphron: Or, The Minute Philosopher*, in *The Works of George Berkeley, Bishop of Cloyne*, ed. A. A. Luce and T. E. Jessop, 9 vols. (London: Nelson, 1948–1957), 3:298; Joseph Butler, "Of Personal Identity," in *The Works of Joseph Butler*, ed. W. E. Gladstone, 2 vols. (Oxford: Clarendon Press, 1896), 1:387 (my italics); and David Hume, *A Treatise of Human Nature*, ed. L. A. Selby-Bigge, rev. P. H. Nidditch (2d ed., Oxford: Clarendon Press, 1978), p. 259.

4. On this point, see Christopher Fox, "Defining Eighteenth-Century Psychology: Some Problems and Perspectives," in *Psychology and Literature in the Eighteenth Century*, ed. Christopher Fox (New York: AMS Studies in the Eighteenth Century, 1987), pp. 1–22.

5. Kerby-Miller in Pope, *The Memoirs of Scriblerus*, p. vii.

1. SOME PROBLEMS OF PERSPECTIVE

1. Ian Watt, *The Rise of the Novel* (Berkeley and Los Angeles: University of California Press, 1957), p. 18. For literary studies that do recognize Locke's importance see especially John A. Dussinger, *The Discourse of the Mind in Eighteenth-Century Fiction* (The Hague: Mouton, 1974), pp. 31–43; and Ernest Lee Tuveson, *The Imagination as a Means of Grace: Locke and the Aesthetics of Romanticism* (Berkeley and Los Angeles: University of California Press, 1960).

2. Ernst Cassirer, *The Philosophy of the Enlightenment*, trans. Fritz C. A. Koelln and James P. Pettegrove (Princeton: Princeton University Press, 1951), p. 99; and Donald Greene, "Augustinianism and Empiricism: A Note on Eighteenth-Century English Intellectual History," *Eighteenth-Century Studies* 1 (1967–1968): 52. For similar statements: Perry Miller, *Errand into the Wilderness* (New York: Harper, 1964), p. 168; and Basil Willey, *The Seventeenth Century Background* (Garden City: Doubleday, 1953), pp. 264–65.

3. Kenneth Maclean, *John Locke and English Literature of the Eighteenth Century* (New Haven: Yale University Press, 1936), pp. 5–6; and John W. Yolton, *John Locke and the Way of Ideas* (Oxford: Clarendon Press, 1956), p. ix.

4. Leo Braudy, "Penetration and Impenetrability in *Clarissa*," in *New Approaches to Eighteenth-Century Literature: Selected Papers from the English Institute*, ed. Phillip Harth (New York: Columbia University Press, 1974), p. 182; Patricia Meyer Spacks, *Imagining a Self: Autobiography and Novel in Eighteenth-Century England* (Cambridge, Mass.: Harvard University Press, 1976), p. 3; David Hume, *A Treatise of Human Nature*, ed. L. A. Selby-Bigge, rev. P. H. Nidditch (2d ed., Oxford: Clarendon Press, 1978), p. 259.

Because the *Treatise* is such a remarkable book, we also tend to forget that in the first decade of its existence the work itself received surprisingly little attention. (This of course would change in the 1760s and thereafter, with the major critiques of Beattie and others.) Quoting Pope, to whom he sent a copy of the *Treatise*, Hume tells us in *My Own Life*: "Never literary attempt was more unfortunate than my Treatise of Human Nature. It fell *dead-born from the press*, without reaching such distinction, as even to excite a murmur among the zealots." Though this statement "by no means tells the whole story," says Hume's modern biographer, "the immediate reception of the *Treatise* was certainly not such as to lend him encouragement." See

Hume's *Philosophical Works*, ed. Thomas H. Green and Thomas H. Grose, 4 vols. (1882–1886; reprint ed., Darmstadt: Scientia Verlag, 1964), 3:2; and Ernest Campbell Mossner, *The Life of David Hume* (Austin: University of Texas Press, 1954), p. 116.

5. Thomas Reid, *Essays on the Intellectual Powers of Man* (1785; reprint ed., New York: Garland Publishing, 1971), pp. 333, 336 (my italics).

6. That Butler is directly alluding to Collins's use of Locke is indicated by Butler's own note to this comment: "See an *Answer to Dr. Clarke's Third Defence*." See "Of Personal Identity," *The Works of Joseph Butler*, ed. W. E. Gladstone, 2 vols. (Oxford: Clarendon Press, 1896), 1:387, 392 (my italics), and 392n.

7. *Two Dissertations Concerning Sense and the Imagination. With an Essay on Consciousness* (London, 1728), pp. 141, 143 (my italics). Nearly a century ago, commenting on this work, Noah Porter noted that it "is surprising that this first and important contribution... has not been better known." With the exception of a Garland reprint (1976), this is still the case. The reprint does not provide an introduction to the *Essay*, nor does it confront the issue of authorship. (The work was not attributed to Mayne until 1824; and Porter later suggested that the author is "probably" the son of a Zachary Mayne who died in 1694. Yet that Mayne had no son of this name. More recently, the work has been attributed to Charles Mayne, though the evidence for his authorship appears, at present, to be slight.) A new edition is being prepared by James G. Buickerood and the present author. See Noah Porter, "Philosophy in Great Britain and America: A Supplementary Sketch," appended to his translation of Friedrich Ueberweg's *A History of Philosophy*, 2 vols. (New York: Scribner's, 1890), 2:368. A computer search of the *Eighteenth-Century Short Title Catalogue* shows only two other works between 1700 and 1800 with the word *consciousness* in a main title: an obscure sermon published in 1727, and a one-page apology in 1770. Both are inconsequential.

8. John Locke, *An Essay Concerning Human Understanding*, ed. P. H. Nidditch (Oxford: Clarendon Press, 1975), p. 345. Hereafter, references in the text to the *Essay* are to this edition and will be given in Arabic numbers in the order book, chapter, section: e.g., 2.27.23. In an extended consideration of some book and chapter, where it is obvious that I am discussing the same chapter, I give only section numbers.

9. See Alexander Campbell Fraser, ed., *An Essay Concerning Human Understanding* (1894; reprint ed., New York: Dover, 1959), 1:448–49n.

10. "*Consciousness* est un mot anglais, auquel j'avoue que je ne trouve point d'équivalent dans notre langue." See *Élémens de la Philosophie de l'Esprit Humain. Par Dugald Stewart*, trans. Pierre Prévost, 2 vols. (Geneva, 1808), "Préface du Traducteur," 1 : xix–xx. For difficulties in finding a French equivalent for the English *consciousness*, see also note 11 below and the Continental review of *An Essay on Consciousness* (London, 1728) in *Bibliotheque Raisonnée des Ouvrages des Savans de l'Europe* 2 (1729): 293–311, especially 308–11.

11. Pierre Coste, trans., *Essai Philosophique Concernant L'Entendement Humain par M. Locke* (5th ed., Amsterdam and Leipzig, 1755), pp. 264–65n. The original reads:

> Le mot Anglois est *consciousness*.... En François nous n'avons à mon avis que les mots de *sentiment* & de *conviction* qui répondent en quelque sorte à cette idée. Mais en plusieurs endroits de ce Chapitre ils ne peuvent qu'exprimer fort imparfaitement la pensée de Mr. *Locke*, qui fait absolument dépendre *l'identité personnelle* de cet acte de l'Homme *quo sibi est conscius*.... Après avoir songé quelque tems aux moyens de remédier à cet inconvénient, je n'en ai point trouvé de meiileur [*sic*] que de me servir du terme de *Conscience* pour exprimer cet acte même. C'est pourquoi j'aurai soin de le faire imprimer en Italique, afin que le Lecteur se souvienne d'y attacher toujours cette idée. Et pour faire qu'on distingue encore mieux cette signification d'avec celle qu'on donne ordinairement à ce mot, il m'est venu dans l'esprit un expédient.... c'est d'écrire *conscience* en deux mots joints par un tiret, de cette maniére, *con-science*. Mais, dira t-on, voilà une étrange licence, de détourner un mot de sa signification ordinaire, pour lui en attribuer une qu'on ne lui a jamais donnée dans notre Langue....J'avoue que dans un Ouvrage qui ne seroit pas, comme celui-ci, de pur raisonnement, une pareille liberté seroit tout-à-fait inexcusable. Mais dans un Discours Philosophique non seulement on peut, mais on doit employer des mots nouveaux ... lorsqu'on n'en a point qui expriment l'idée *précise* de l'Auteur.

The same note appears, in slightly altered form, in the first edition (1700).

12. Coste, *Essai*, p. 265n, refers the reader to book 3, part 2, chapter 7, section 4 of the *Recherche*, a section titled "Comment on connaît son âme." Right at the beginning of this section, Malebranche says:

> Il n'en est pas de même de l'ame, nous ne la connoissons point par son idée: nous ne la voïons point en Dieu: nous ne la connoissons que par *conscience*.

Malebranche's most recent translators render it this way:

> Such is not the case with the soul, [which] we do not know through its idea—we do not see it in God; we know it only through *consciousness.*

The earliest English translators, however, do not make this switch. *Conscience* remains "conscience"; and the word *consciousness* is conspicuously absent. The earliest English translator, for instance, tells us:

> It is not so with the Soul, we do not know it by its Idea: We do not see it in God; we only know it by *Conscience.*

The second translator, Thomas Taylor, likewise says:

> But 'tis not so in point of the Soul; we know her not by her Idea; we see her not in GOD; we know her only by Conscience.

See Nicolas Malebranche, *Recherche de la vérité,* ed. Geneviève Rodis-Lewis, 3 vols. (Paris: J. Vrin, 1945–1962), 1:451; *The Search after Truth,* trans. Thomas M. Lennon and Paul J. Olscamp (Columbus: Ohio State University Press, 1980), p. 237; *Malebranch's Search After Truth ... Done out of French from the last Edition,* [trans. Richard Sault], 2 vols. (London, 1694–1695), 1:57; and *Father Malebranche's Treatise Concerning the Search After Truth,* trans. Thomas Taylor (London, 1694), p. 125. I thank James Buickerood for calling this to my attention.

13. See Yolton, *Way of Ideas,* pp. 22–24. Coste began his translation in 1696 under the encouragement of Jean Le Clerc, editor of the highly respected *Bibliothèque Universelle*; Coste completed it at Oates, where he served from 1697 on as a tutor to the Mashams and a secretary to Locke himself. See Maurice Cranston, *John Locke: A Biography* (New York: Macmillan, 1957), p. 438; and Locke, *Essay,* ed. Nidditch, pp. xxxiv–xxxvi. Information about Locke and Coste also appears in Joseph Spence, *Observations, Anecdotes, and Characters of Books and Men,* ed. James M. Osborn, 2 vols. (Oxford: Clarendon Press, 1966), 2:560, No. 1502.

14. One name absent from Coste's note is Descartes. This is surprising, for the usual story has it that Descartes essentially invented the concept of consciousness. If consciousness was so important to Descartes, why does Coste fail to mention him? Is it because Descartes himself never really defined the term and rarely used it? Perhaps so. Some years ago, Alfred Balz noted that the standard story needs to be revised, for it is "difficult ... to credit Descartes himself with this doc-

trine." What was important to Descartes was the soul's "capacity of reasoning...not self-consciousness." See Alfred G. A. Balz, *Cartesian Studies* (New York: Columbia University Press, 1951), pp. 29, 40. Coste's failure to mention Descartes may also be connected with another point: that in seventeenth-century *French* translations of Descartes's Latin, his uses of the Latin *conscientia* are most often rendered as "sentiment" or "connoissance"; the word *conscience* is, apparently, used just once. On this point, see Robert McRae, "Descartes' Definition of Thought," in *Cartesian Studies*, ed. R. J. Butler (Oxford: Basil Blackwell, 1972), p. 55n. In the history of the concept of consciousness, Locke's place is (one suspects) more important than usually noticed.

15. Amélie Oskenberg Rorty, "A Literary Postscript: Characters, Persons, Selves, Individuals," in *The Identities of Persons*, ed. Amélie Oskenberg Rorty (Berkeley and Los Angeles: University of California Press, 1976), p. 309. For earlier concepts of the substantial self, see especially Sir Ronald Syme's *Tacitus*, 2 vols. (Oxford: Clarendon Press, 1958), 1:420–21; and R. G. Collingwood, *The Idea of History* (Oxford: Clarendon Press, 1946), pp. 42–45.

16. Boethius, *The Theological Tractates*, trans. H. F. Stewart and E. K. Rand (London: Loeb Classical Library, 1918), p. 92; Étienne Gilson, "Christian Personalism," in *The Spirit of Mediaeval Philosophy*, trans. A. C. H. Downes (New York: Scribner's, 1940), p. 201; and John Clendon, *Tractatus Philosophico-Theologicus de Persona. Or, A Treatise of the Word Person* (London, 1710), p. 94.

17. John Smith, *A Discourse Demonstrating the Immortality of the Soul*, in his *Select Discourses* (London, 1660), p. 66.

18. Sir John Davies, *Nosce Teipsum*, in *Silver Poets of the Sixteenth Century*, ed. Gerald Bullet (London: Everyman, 1947), pp. 362, 397.

19. Ralph Cudworth, *The True Intellectual System of the Universe* (London, 1678), p. 868.

20. Gilson, "Christian Personalism," p. 203.

21. Samuel Clarke, *The Works of Samuel Clarke*, 4 vols. (London, 1738), 3:851.

22. René Descartes, *Philosophical Writings*, trans. John Cottingham, Robert Stoothoff, and Dugald Murdoch, 2 vols. (Cambridge, England: Cambridge University Press, 1985), 1:127.

23. In the *Second Meditation*, Descartes posits: "Thinking? At last I have discovered it—thought; this alone is inseparable from me. I am, I exist—that is certain. But for how long? For as long as I am thinking. For it could be that were I totally to cease from thinking, I should

totally cease to exist." In the *Sixth Meditation*, he argues "that there is a great difference between the mind and the body, inasmuch as the body is by its very nature always divisible, while the mind is utterly indivisible." See the *Philosophical Writings*, 2:18, 59.

24. Wolfgang von Leyden, *Seventeenth-Century Metaphysics: An Examination of Some Main Concepts and Theories* (New York: Barnes and Noble, 1968), p. 111; and Henry E. Allison, "Locke's Theory of Personal Identity: A Re-Examination," in *Locke on Human Understanding: Selected Essays*, ed. I. C. Tipton (Oxford: Clarendon Press, 1977), p. 106.

25. Joseph Wood Krutch, *"Modernism" in Modern Drama: A Definition and an Estimate* (Ithaca: Cornell University Press, 1953), p. 83; and Tuveson, *Imagination*, pp. 27–29.

26. Anthony Collins, *An Answer to Mr. Clarke's Third Defence*, in *Works of Clarke*, 3:870; and Samuel Clarke, *A Third Defence of An Argument Made Use of in a Letter to Mr. Dodwell*, in Clarke, *Works of Clarke*, 3:844. Also see Clarke's comments in *A Fourth Defence of An Argument Made Use of in a Letter to Mr. Dodwell*, in Clarke, *Works of Clarke*, 3:902.

27. Dugald Stewart, *The Collected Works*, ed. Sir William Hamilton, 11 vols. (Edinburgh, 1854), 1:604; and *Berkeley and Percival*, ed. B. Rand (Cambridge, England: Cambridge University Press, 1914), pp. 114, 121, 123. When Berkeley called Arbuthnot "a great philosopher" we must also remember the possibility that he may have meant "natural philosopher," or what we call a scientist.

28. *The Correspondence of Jonathan Swift*, ed. Sir Harold Williams, 5 vols. (Oxford: Clarendon Press, 1963–1965), 2:137.

29. See Swift's *Remarks upon a Book, Intitled, The Rights of the Christian Church*, in *The Prose Works of Jonathan Swift*, ed. Herbert Davis, 14 vols. (Oxford: Basil Blackwell, 1938–1968), 2:80. That Swift employed the controversy over Locke has been argued by Rosalie Colie, Irvin Ehrenpreis, and W. B. Carnochan. Though the first two studies nominally deal with personal identity, they actually take up the related, though different, issue of defining the essence of "man" as "species"— a point Carnochan's book clarifies. See Rosalie L. Colie, "Gulliver, the Locke-Stillingfleet Controversy, and the Nature of Man," *History of Ideas News Letter* 2 (1956): 58–62; Irvin Ehrenpreis, "The Meaning of Gulliver's Last Voyage," in *Swift: A Collection of Critical Essays*, ed. Ernest Lee Tuveson (Englewood Cliffs, N. J.: Prentice-Hall, 1964), pp. 123–42; and W. B. Carnochan, *Lemuel Gulliver's Mirror for Man*

(Berkeley and Los Angeles: University of California Press, 1968), esp. pp. 130–31, 150–53. Also see Ricardo Quintana, *Two Augustans: John Locke, Jonathan Swift* (Madison: University of Wisconsin Press, 1978).

30. Ernest Lee Tuveson, "*An Essay on Man* and 'The Way of Ideas,'" *English Literary History* 26 (1959): 368–69.

31. On Pope's copy of Locke's *Essay*, see Maynard Mack, "Pope's Books: A Biographical Survey with a Finding List," in *English Literature in the Age of Disguise*, ed. Maximillian Novak (Berkeley and Los Angeles: University of California Press, 1977), p. 271, item no. 105. For Pope's comments on Locke, see Spence's *Anecdotes*, 1:92, no. 212; 170–71, nos. 388–89; p. 217, no. 510; p. 226, no. 535.

32. In a note to *The Dunciad*, Pope tells us that in "the year 1703 there was a meeting of the heads of Oxford to censure Mr. Locke's Essay on Human Understanding, and to forbid the reading of it." As Maurice Cranston shows, the details of this censure were shadowy, even to Locke himself. Locke's friends were, however, able to establish that such meetings did in fact take place in November 1703; that they were directed primarily at Locke's *Essay* and Le Clerc's *Logic*; and that the attempt failed. See *The Twickenham Edition of the Works of Alexander Pope*, ed. John Butt, 11 vols. (New Haven: Yale University Press, 1939–1969), vol. 5, *The Dunciad*, ed. James Sutherland (3d ed., 1963), p. 361n. Also see Cranston, *John Locke*, pp. 466–69.

33. Maclean, *John Locke and English Literature*, pp. 10–11, 101; and William Warburton, *The Works of Alexander Pope, Esq.*, 9 vols. (London, 1751), 6:127, 129. See also Robert A. Erickson, "Situations of Identity in *The Memoirs of Martinus Scriblerus*," *Modern Language Quarterly* 26 (1965): 388–400; and A. C. Fraser's edition of Locke's *Essay*, 1:455n.

34. A. C. Lloyd, "On Augustine's Concept of a Person," in *Augustine: A Collection of Critical Essays*, ed. R. A. Markus (New York: Anchor, 1972), p. 191. Also see p. 197.

35. Thomas Aquinas, *Summa contra Gentiles: Book Four*, trans. Charles J. O'Neil (Notre Dame, Ind.: University of Notre Dame Press, 1975), chapters 80–81, pp. 301, 303.

36. Robert Boyle, *Some Physico-Theological Considerations about the Possibility of the Resurrection*, in *Selected Philosophical Papers of Robert Boyle*, ed. M. A. Stewart (Manchester: Manchester University Press, 1979), pp. xxiii, 206. That in the early eighteenth century the problem was still seen as closely related to traditional doctrines is suggested by Isaac Watts's careful note to his attack on Locke's theory in 1733:

"This discourse is entirely confined to personality among creatures, and has no reference to divine personality here." ("Of Identity and Diversity," in *Philosophical Essays on Various Subjects ... with Some Remarks on Mr. Locke's Essay on the Human Understanding* [London, 1733], in *The Works*, ed. George Burder, 6 vols. [London, 1810–1811], 5:624n.)

37. On the connection between Locke and the Deists, see Yolton, *Way of Ideas*, esp. pp. 126–48, 167–81. One question that could use more exploration is the connection between Locke's theory in 1694 and the Trinitarian controversy of the same decade.

38. Other works that take up Locke's theory within the traditional context of these theological concerns include, for example, Henry Lee, *Anti-Scepticism: Or, Notes upon each Chapter of Mr. Lock's Essay concerning Humane Understanding* (London, 1702); [Samuel Bold], *A Discourse concerning the Resurrection of the Same Body* (London, 1705); Will Lupton, *The Resurrection of the Same Body: A Sermon Preach'd before the University of Oxford* (Oxford, 1711); Winch Holdsworth's sequel to his anti-Lockean sermon of 1720, *A Defence of the Doctrine of the Resurrection of the Same Body ... in which the Character, Writings, and Religious Principles of Mr. Lock ... are Distinctly considered* (London, 1727); Catherine Trotter [Cockburn], *A Letter to Dr. Holdsworth, in Vindication of Mr. Locke* (London, 1726); Henry Felton, *The Universality ... of the Resurrection, being a Sequel to that wherein Personal Identity is asserted* (London, 1733); and Isaac Watts, "The Resurrection of the Same Body," in *Philosophical Essays on Various Subjects* (1733), in *The Works*, 5:576–80.

39. Locke, *Essay*, p. 11. Yolton has shown that it was Locke's interest in solving such problems that initially led to the formation of his new way of ideas. See Yolton, *Way of Ideas*, esp. p. viii.

2. STRANGE SUPPOSITIONS

1. *The Correspondence of John Locke*, ed. E. S. DeBeer, 8 vols. (Oxford: Clarendon Press, 1976), 4:623.

2. In the dedication prefixed to his *Dioptrica Nova: A Treatise of Dioptricks* (London, 1692), Molyneux, who did not know the philosopher at the time, praised "the incomparable Mr. *Locke*, Who, in his *Essay* ... has rectified more received Mistakes, and delivered more profound Truths, established on Experience and Observation, for the Direction of Man's mind in the Prosecution of Knowledge ... than are to be met with in all the Volumes of the Antients" (p. [iv]). Two years later, in a letter dated 18 December 1694, Molyneux would also recommend to Locke "a very Worthy Person, Dr St George Ashe

Provost of the Colledge here." See Locke's *Correspondence*, 5:243. For Swift's relationship with Ashe, which was close, see Irvin Ehrenpreis's *Swift: The Man, His Works, and the Age*, 3 vols. (Cambridge Mass.: Harvard University Press, 1962–1983), 1:47, 51–56.

3. Locke's *Correspondence*, 4:647, 650, 665, 722. When Molyneux requested a chapter on the "Principium Individuationis" he may have had in mind recent treatments of that older issue by writers such as Hobbes. In a brief discussion of "the beginning of *individuation*," Hobbes, incidentally, seems at one point to anticipate Locke's view of human identity as an equivocal term: "For it is one thing to ask concerning Socrates, whether he be the same man, and another to ask whether he be the same body; for his body, when he is old, cannot be the same it was when he was an infant... yet... he may be the same man." Despite this statement, in a chapter (teasingly) titled "Of Identity and Difference," Hobbes's concern here is of course with bodily identity rather than personal identity in a Lockean sense. See the *Elements of Philosophy*, in *The English Works of Thomas Hobbes*, ed. Sir William Molesworth, 11 vols. (London, 1839), 1:137.

4. For Locke's comments on the "storm" against the *Essay*, see his later letter to Molyneux on 11 September 1697 in Locke's *Correspondence*, 6:191. For Molyneux's comments on Locke's earlier mention of personal identity, see Locke's *Correspondence*, 4:650.

5. That Locke was thinking specifically about personal identity as early as 1683 is suggested by an unpublished journal entry for that year. See his comments in the Lovelace Collection (MS. Locke f. 7, p. 107) for 5 June 1683, quoted in Kenneth Dewhurst's *John Locke (1632–1704), Physician and Philosopher: A Medical Biography* (London: Wellcome Historical Medical Library, 1963), pp. 222–23. In *Locke: An Introduction* (Oxford: Basil Blackwell, 1985), John W. Yolton has seen the concept of person as increasingly central to Locke's thought on any number of subjects.

6. See Locke's entry for 21 February 1682 in *An Early Draft of Locke's Essay, Together with Excerpts from His Journals*, ed. R. I. Aaron and Jocelyn Gibb (Oxford: Clarendon Press, 1936), pp. 123–25. The *cogito* is echoed throughout the *Essay*. "If I doubt of all other Things," Locke notes at one point, "that very doubt makes me perceive my own *Existence*" (4.9.3). "'Tis past controversy," he says at another, "that we have in us something that thinks, our very Doubts about what it is, confirm the certainty of its being, though [and this is where he departs from Descartes] we must content our selves in the Ignorance of what kind of *Being* it is" (4.3.6).

7. Isaac Watts, "Of Identity and Diversity," in *Philosophical Essays on Various Subjects . . . with Some Remarks on Mr. Locke's Essay on the Human Understanding* (London, 1733), in *The Works*, ed. George Burder, 6 vols. (London, 1810–1811), 5:629. For Locke's characterization of himself, see his *Correspondence*, 4:665.

8. Henry E. Allison, "Locke on Personal Identity: A Re-Examination," in *Locke on the Human Understanding*, ed. I. C. Tipton (Oxford: Clarendon Press, 1977), p. 105. For a similar statement of Locke's originality, see Ben Lazare Misjuskovic, who asserts in *The Achilles of Rationalist Arguments* (The Hague: Nijhoff, 1974) that Locke "introduces the question of personal identity into philosophy" (p. 95).

9. In 2.1 of the *Essay*, Locke devotes nine sections to proving that "the soul always thinks" is not a self-evident proposition. "I confess my self, to have one of those dull Souls," Locke argues, "that doth not perceive it self always to contemplate *Ideas*, nor can conceive it any more necessary for the *Soul always to think*, than for the Body always to move; the perception of *Ideas* being . . . to the Soul, what motion is to the Body, not its Essence, but one of its Operations" (2.1.10).

10. In his chapter "*Of Our Complex* Idea *of Substance*," Locke comments that "*the Idea we have of Spirit, compared with the Idea* we have *of Body*, stands thus: The substance of Spirit is unknown to us; and so is the substance of Body, equally unknown to us" (2.23.30). Also see 2.23.5.

11. In 4.3.6, Locke claims that we know so little of our souls that it is conceivable "that GOD can, if he pleases, superadd to Matter a Faculty of Thinking . . . since we know not wherein Thinking consists." This comment sparked the extensive "thinking matter" controversy, which often runs parallel to the contemporary debate over personal identity. For details, see John W. Yolton, *Thinking Matter: Materialism in Eighteenth-Century Britain* (Minneapolis: University of Minnesota Press, 1983). Bolingbroke later evokes this idea when he asks whether the "faculty of thinking" may "have been superadded by omnipotence to certain systems of matter." See *The Philosophical Works of the late Right Honorable Henry St. John, Viscount Bolingbroke*, 5 vols. (London, 1754), 1:21. For the questions about the persistence of the soul, see Allison, "Locke," p. 107.

12. Allison, "Locke," p. 107.

13. Irvin Ehrenpreis, "The Meaning of Gulliver's Last Voyage," in *Swift: A Collection of Critical Essays*, ed. Ernest Lee Tuveson (Englewood Cliffs, N.J.: Prentice-Hall, 1964), p. 132. The example Swift transcribed for Temple found its way not only into Locke's chapter but

also into other works. See, for example, Richard Burthogge, *An Essay Upon Reason and the Nature of Spirits* (London, 1694), pp. 18–22.

14. My aim is to chart, not twentieth-century interpretations of Locke's theory, but eighteenth-century views. If we wished, however, to get a sense of the range of current discussion, we might look, for instance, at Sydney Shoemaker's and Richard Swinburne's volume in The Great Debates in Philosophy series, *Personal Identity* (Oxford: Basil Blackwell, 1984); at Derek Parfit's *Reasons and Persons* (Oxford: Clarendon Press, 1984); or at recent volumes of *The Locke Newsletter*. An earlier (though still helpful) bibliography of works on the larger issue is available in Amélie Oskenberg Rorty, ed., *The Identities of Persons* (Berkeley and Los Angeles: University of California Press, 1976), pp. 325–33.

For our purposes, which are historical, an important piece of recent scholarship is David P. Behan's "Locke on Persons and Personal Identity," *Canadian Journal of Philosophy* 9 (1979): 53–75. Also of help here: Udo Thiel, "Locke's Concept of a Person," in *John Locke: Symposium, Wolfenbüttel, 1979,* ed. Reinhard Brandt (Berlin: Walter de Gruyter, 1981), pp. 173–203; and Thiel's *Lockes Theorie der personalen Identität* (Bonn: Bouvier, 1983).

15. Vincent Perronet, *A Second Vindication of Mr. Locke, Wherein his Sentiments relating to Personal Identity are clear'd from some Mistakes of the Rev. Dr. Butler, in his Dissertation on that Subject* (London, 1738), p. 21. Before this work, Perronet had earlier defended Locke, this time against Peter Browne, in *A Vindication of Mr. Locke* (London, 1736). Perronet (1693–1785), the vicar of Shoreham, later came under the influence of the Methodists; he is perhaps best known to posterity for the riot in his church on the day he allowed Charles Wesley to preach.

16. That is, it is one thing for Jones to be conscious today of stealing Jackson's wallet yesterday; it is another for Jones to be *concerned* about that theft, morally to appropriate that act as his own. As David Behan points out: "To assume [as most have] that Locke used 'consciousness' as more or less equivalent to 'memory' is to overlook a functional distinction which Locke made between memory and concerned consciousness. While memory allows one access to past perceptions, it is through concerned consciousness that they are appropriated as one's own." ("Locke on Persons," p. 66. Also see Thiel, "Locke's Concept of a Person," p. 188.)

A tendency to confuse such terms has marred attempts at a history of Locke's concept. See, for instance, R. C. Tennant, "The Anglican

Response to Locke's Theory of Personal Identity," *Journal of the History of Ideas* 43 (1982): 73–90.

17. On this point, see Anthony Flew, "Locke and the Problem of Personal Identity," in *Locke and Berkeley: A Collection of Critical Essays*, ed. C. B. Martin and D. M. Armstrong (Notre Dame, Ind.: University of Notre Dame Press, 1968), pp. 156–57.

18. [Catherine Trotter Cockburn], *A Defence of The Essay of Human Understanding, Written by Mr. Lock* (London, 1702), p. 66.

3. OF PORCUPINES, PROBLEMS, AND MORE PROBLEMS

1. For some later comments, which tend to return to issues raised earlier, see Henry Home, Lord Kames, *Essays on the Principles of Morality and Natural Religion* (2d ed., rev., London, 1758), pp. 189–92; [Abraham Tucker], *Man in Quest of Himself: Or A Defence of the Individuality of the Human Mind, or Self* (London, 1763); Joseph Priestley, *Disquisitions Relating to Matter and Spirit* (London, 1777), pp. 155–66; [Edmund Law], *A Defence of Mr. Locke's Opinion concerning Personal Identity* (1769) in *The Works of John Locke*, 10 vols. (1823; reprint ed., Darmstadt, Scientia Verlag, 1963), 3:179–201; and Thomas Reid, *Essays on the Intellectual Powers of Man* (1785; reprint ed., New York: Garland Publishing, 1971).

2. Thomas Burnet, *Remarks upon An Essay Concerning Humane Understanding. In a Letter to the Author* (London, 1697), pp. 12–13.

3. Henry Lee, *Anti-Scepticism: Or, Notes upon each Chapter of Mr. Lock's Essay Concerning Humane Understanding* (London, 1702), pp. 124, 130.

4. Edward Stillingfleet, *The Bishop of Worcester's Answer to Mr. Locke's Second Letter, Wherein his Notion of Ideas Is prov'd to be Inconsistent with it self And with the Articles of the Christian Faith* (London, 1698), pp. 59, 175.

5. Lee, *Anti-Scepticism*, p. 128.

6. Jacob Viner, "Man's Economic Status," in *Man versus Society in Eighteenth-Century Britain*, ed. James Clifford (New York: W. W. Norton, 1972), p. 34.

7. Joseph M. Levine, *Dr. Woodward's Shield: History, Science, and Satire in Augustan England* (Berkeley and Los Angeles: University of California Press, 1977), p. 136. Molyneux's remark appears in a letter to Locke, 4 October 1697, in *The Correspondence of John Locke*, ed. E. S. DeBeer, 8 vols. (Oxford: Clarendon Press, 1976), 6:220.

8. Richard Popkin, "The Philosophy of Bishop Stillingfleet," *Journal of the History of Philosophy* 9 (1971): 311. On Stillingfleet's thought, also see R. T. Carroll's *The Common-Sense Philosophy of Religion of Bishop Edward Stillingfleet* (The Hague: Nijhoff, 1975).

9. Edward Stillingfleet, *Discourse in Vindication of the Doctrine of the Trinity* (London, 1696), pp. 234, 252, 242, 261.

10. See Locke's letter to Limborch, 29 October 1697, in Maurice Cranston, *John Locke: A Biography* (New York: Macmillan, 1957), p. 429; and Locke's *Correspondence*, 6:244–45.

11. John Locke, *A Letter to the Right Reverend Edward Ld Bishop of Worcester, concerning some Passages relating to Mr. Locke's Essay of Humane Understanding: In a late Discourse of his Lordships, in Vindication of the Trinity* (London, 1697), pp. 10–11, 40, 32.

12. Stillingfleet, *Answer to Mr. Locke's Second Letter*, pp. 35–36, 171, 172–73.

13. Lee, *Anti-Scepticism*, pp. 129–30.

14. Ibid., pp. 125, 130.

15. John Sergeant, *Solid Philosophy Asserted, Against the Fancies of the Ideists ... with Reflexions on Mr. Locke's Essay Concerning Human Understanding* (London, 1697), pp. 265–66.

16. George Berkeley, *The Works of George Berkeley, Bishop of Cloyne*, ed. A. A. Luce and T. E. Jessop, 9 vols. (London: Nelson, 1948–1957), 1:87, no. 713; p. 64, no. 517; and p. 86, no. 700. for a helpful modern assessment, see S. C. Brown, "Berkeley on the Unity of the Self," in *Reason and Reality*, ed. G. N. A. Vesey (London: Macmillan, 1972), pp. 64–87.

17. Luce notes that Berkeley dropped *person* perhaps "Because of its ecclesiastical associations" and that it is never used in *The Principles*. See the Works, 1:107n, 134n.

18. George Berkeley, *Three Dialogues Between Hylas and Philonous*, in *Works*, 2:233–34.

19. Joseph Butler, "Of Personal Identity," in *The Works of Joseph Butler*, ed. W. E. Gladstone, 2 vols. (Oxford: Clarendon Press, 1896), 1:388, 395–96.

20. Butler, *Works*, 1:387.

21. Reid, *Essays*, p. 336.

22. Sergeant, *Solid Philosophy Asserted*, p. 263.

23. Lee, *Anti-Scepticism*, pp. 124, 128, 127.

24. "As for them that place *Thinking* in a purely material Animal Constitution void of Spirit," argues Lee, Locke "reckons them sure of

his side, that *Consciousness* only makes *Personal Identity....* But I can tell him, that if the fleeting Animal Spirits, be the *Soul*, the Intelligent Being; there will be as many *Persons* as there are distinct Animal *Spirits* or Particles of *refin'd* Matter. For with all their jostling one another they can never make each other *conscious* of their several Motions or Actions: and so for one *Person* we may have such a *numerous* Club of them as all the Ventricles of the Brain can hold; and as often as they *change*, which 'tis likely is almost every Moment of Life, at least as often as the man takes a Nod, there may be Persons enough to people the world, in every single Body, without going to the Moon or the rest of the Planets for Inhabitants." (*Anti-Scepticism,* p. 125.)

25. *The Guardian,* ed. John Calhoun Stephens (Lexington: University of Kentucky Press, 1982), p. 49. Also cited in *The Memoirs of Martinus Scriblerus,* p. 284n.

26. Samuel Clarke, *The Works of Samuel Clarke,* 4 vols. (London, 1738), 3:889. The Clarke-Collins controversy generated nine book-length pamphlets between 1706 and 1708, all of which are reprinted in this volume of Clarke's *Works,* 3:719–913. For economy's sake, all further references to the debate are to this edition, cited in the text by page number only.

The original pamphlets are as follows: Clarke, *A Letter to Mr. Dodwell, wherein all the Arguments in his Epistolary Discourse against the Immortality of the Soul are particularly answered* (London, 1706); Collins, *A Letter to the learned Mr. Henry Dodwell: Containing some Remarks on a (pretended) Demonstration of the Immateriality and Natural Immortality of the Soul* (London, 1706); Clarke, *A Defence of an Argument made use of in a Letter to Mr. Dodwell* (London, 1707); Collins, *A Reply to Mr. Clarke's Defence* (London, 1707); Clarke, *A Second Defence* (London, 1707); Collins, *Reflections on Mr. Clarke's Second Defence* (London, 1707); Clarke, *A Third Defence* (London, 1707); Collins, *An Answer to Mr. Clarke's Third Defence* (London, 1708); and Clarke's *A Fourth Defence* (London, 1708).

27. Henry Dodwell's tract is entitled *An Epistolary Discourse proving from the Scriptures and the first Fathers that the Soul is a principle Naturally Mortal, but immortalized actually by the Pleasure of God* (London, 1706). As his title indicates, Dodwell argues that the soul is naturally mortal, until immortalized by baptism. James Ferguson's estimate of the role Dodwell plays in the ensuing debate between Clarke and Collins is accurate: "Apart from the opening exchanges, Dodwell is not mentioned. He takes no part in the controversy, which becomes a straight-

forward duel between Clarke and Collins." (James P. Ferguson, *The Philosophy of Dr. Samuel Clarke and Its Critics* [New York: Vantage Press, 1974], p. 139.) Though there is a recent essay on Clarke's concept of personal identity, modern scholarship on the whole offers little help here. See Howard M. Ducharme, "Personal Identity in Samuel Clarke," *Journal of the History of Philosophy* 24 (1986): 359–83.

28. *Works of Clarke*, 3:851–52. For a similar argument, see Stillingfleet, *Answer to Mr. Locke's Second Letter*, pp. 34–43.

29. See James O'Higgins's bibliography in his *Anthony Collins: The Man and His Works* (The Hague: Nijhoff, 1970), p. 244.

30. Butler, *Works*, 1:392n, 392–93.

31. Butler, *Works*, 1:393. Vincent Perronet would accuse Butler, two years later, of failing to distinguish "between Mr. *Locke*, and those who have made a very absurd and wicked Use, of what is said by him [on] this Subject." See Vincent Perronet's *Second Vindication of Mr. Locke, Wherein his Sentiments relating to Personal Identity are clear'd from some Mistakes of the Rev. Dr. Butler, in his Dissertation on that Subject* (London, 1738), p. 1.

32. David Hume, *A Treatise of Human Nature*, ed. L. A. Selby-Bigge, rev. P. H. Nidditch (2d ed., Oxford: Clarendon Press, 1978), p. 259; and Isaac Watts, "Of Identity and Diversity," in *Philosophical Essays on Various Subjects . . . with Some Remarks on Mr. Locke's Essay on the Human Understanding* (London, 1733), in *The Works*, ed. George Burder, 6 vols. (London, 1810–1811), 5:625, 629.

33. Butler, *Works*, 1:393.

34. *Dictionary of National Biography*, s.v. "Chambers, Ephraim."

35. Levine, *Dr. Woodward's Shield*, p. 103.

36. John Harris, *Lexicon Technicum: or, An Universal English Dictionary of Arts and Sciences*, 2 vols. (London, 1704–1710), s.v. "Identity."

37. Ephraim Chambers, *Cyclopaedia: Or, An Universal Dictionary of Arts and Sciences*, 2 vols. (London, 1728), s.v. "Identity." Though Chambers has been a neglected figure, the importance of his work cannot be denied. The French *Encyclopédie* began as a translation of Chambers; and a number of his entries passed unnoticed into the *Encyclopédie* and remain there to this day, often under the signature of d'Alembert. See John Lough, *The Encyclopédie* (Newcastle-upon-Tyne: Oriel, 1970), pp. 3, 71.

38. Chambers, *Cyclopaedia*, 1:xxix, i.

39. Hume, *Treatise*, p. 635.

40. The phrase is Henry Lee's, from *Anti-Scepticism*, p. 125.

41. Ibid., p. 127.

42. *Two Dissertations concerning Sense and the Imagination. With An Essay on Consciousness* (London, 1728), p. 149.

43. Perronet, *Second Vindication of Mr. Locke*, p. 9. Shaftesbury also invokes the madman puzzle when he exclaims in "Advice to an Author": "What! talk to myself like some madman, in different persons, and under different characters!" See Anthony, Earl of Shaftesbury, *Characteristics of Men, Manners, Opinions, Times*, ed. J. M. Robertson, 2 vols. (1900; reprint ed., Gloucester, Mass.: Peter Smith, 1963), 1:207.

44. George Berkeley, *Alciphron: Or, The Minute Philosopher*, in *Works*, 3:298–99. The proof that came to be called the "Gallant Officer" appears on 3:299. Thomas Reid later develops it in *Essays*, pp. 333–34:

> Suppose a brave officer to have been flogged when a boy at school, for robbing an orchard, to have taken a standard from the enemy in his first campaign, and to have been made a general in advanced life: Suppose also...that when he took the standard, he was conscious of his having been flogged at school, and that when made a general he was conscious of his taking the standard, but had absolutely lost the consciousness of his flogging.
>
> These things being supposed, it follows, from Mr. Locke's doctrine, that he who was flogged at school is the same person who took the standard, and that he who took the standard is the same person who was made a general. Whence it follows...that the general is the same person with him who was flogged at school. But the general's consciousness does not reach so far back as his flogging, therefore, according to Mr Locke's doctrine, he is not the same person who was flogged. Therefore the general is, and at the same time is not the same person with him who was flogged at school.

45. Watts, *Philosophical Essays on Various Subjects*, in *The Works*, 5:626, 627–28. "Every man, acquainted with the common principles of human action," said Johnson of Watts, "will look with veneration on the writer who is at one time combating Locke, and at another making a catechism for children in their fourth year." See James Boswell's *Life of Johnson*, ed. G. B. Hill, rev. L. F. Powell, 6 vols. (Oxford: Clarendon Press, 1934), 2:408n.

46. Watts, *The Works*, 5:624.

47. Locke's *Correspondence*, 4:767, 785, 5:21, 58.

48. *The Spectator*, ed. D. F. Bond, 5 vols. (Oxford: Clarendon Press, 1965), 4:575–79.

49. Richard Burthogge, *An Essay Upon Reason and the Nature of Spirits* (London, 1694), pp. 264–65.

50. *Aristotle's Masterpiece* (London, 1700), p. 34. This example appears in a chapter titled "Of Monsters, and Monstrous Births," which asks (pp.40–41), among other things, "*whether those that are born Monsters have reasonable Souls, and are capable of a Resurrection?*"

51. Leslie Fiedler, *Freaks: Myths and Images of the Secret Self* (New York: Simon and Schuster, 1978), p. 203.

52. See the account of these twins in *Memoirs of Scriblerus*, ed. Kerby-Miller, p. 295n.

53. *The Correspondence of Jonathan Swift*, ed. Sir Harold Williams, 5 vols. (Oxford: Clarendon Press, 1963–1965), 1:82.

54. *The British Apollo: Containing about Two Thousand Answers To Curious Questions In Most Arts and Sciences* (London, 1711), pp. 292, 246, 258, 482.

4. ON A "METAPHYSICAL GOE-CART"

1. David Hume, *A Treatise of Human Nature*, ed. L. A. Selby-Bigge, rev. P. H. Nidditch (2d ed., Oxford: Clarendon Press, 1978), p. 259.

2. On Clarke's reputation, see A. O. Lovejoy, *The Great Chain of Being* (Cambridge, Mass.: Harvard University Press, 1936), p. 149.

3. Robert Whytt, *An Essay on the Vital and Other Involuntary Motions of Animals* (Edinburgh, 1751), p. 281.

4. Samuel Johnson, *Johnsonian Miscellanies*, ed. G. B. Hill, 2 vols. (1897; reprint ed., New York: Barnes and Noble, 1970), 2:305. To his dying day, Johnson was an avid reader of Samuel Clarke. For some connections between Johnson and Clarke, see James Gray, *Johnson's Sermons: A Study* (Oxford: Clarendon Press, 1972), pp. 65–92; and Robert G. Walker, *Eighteenth-Century Arguments for Immortality and Johnson's "Rasselas"* (Victoria: University of Victoria, 1977). Also of help here is Gwin J. Kolb's "The Intellectual Background of the Discourse of the Soul in *Rasselas*," *Philological Quarterly* 54 (1975): 357–69, esp. 361–63.

5. John Maxwell, "A Summary of the Controversy between Dr. Samuel Clarke and an anonymous Author," in Cumberland's *A Treatise of the Laws of Nature*, trans. John Maxwell (London, 1727), Appendix 1, pp. 1–36; and *A Catalogue of the Capital Well-Known Library of Books of the Late Celebrated Dr. Arbuthnot* (1779; reprint ed., Los Angeles:

William Andrews Clark Memorial Library, Augustan Reprint Society No. 154, 1972), p. 6, no. 71. The Clarke-Collins controversy also comes up in the more famous duel between Clarke and Leibniz: see *The Leibniz-Clarke Correspondence*, ed. H. G. Alexander (Manchester: Manchester University Press, 1956), p. 191.

6. Vincent Perronet, *A Second Vindication of Mr. Locke, Wherein his Sentiments relating to Personal Identity are clear'd from some Mistakes of the Rev. Dr. Butler, in his Dissertation on that Subject* (London, 1738), pp. 1, 17.

7. Bernard Mandeville, *A Treatise of the Hypochondriack and Hysteric Passions* (2d ed., London, 1730), p. 51.

8. By the end of her eighteenth year, Catherine Trotter (1679–1749) had written and staged two plays, the second of which, *The Fatal Friendship*, was highly esteemed by George Farquhar and John Hughes of *Siege of Damascus* fame. When she was twenty-two, she wrote *A Defence of the Essay of Human Understanding, Written by Mr. Lock* (London, 1702) against Thomas Burnet, a work which brought a letter of thanks from John Locke. She then married, raised a family, and was later provoked by Holdsworth's attack to publish another defense of Locke in 1726. After Holdsworth counterattacked in 1727, she wrote a reply, *A Vindication of Mr. Locke's Christian Principles, from the Injurious Imputations of Dr. Holdsworth*, which remained unpublished until her posthumous *Works* in 1751. See *Biographia Britannica* (2d ed., London, 1778), s.v. "Cockburn, Catherine Trotter."

9. Henry Felton, *The Resurrection of the same Numerical Body and its Reunion to the same Soul; Asserted in a Sermon . . . before the University of Oxford . . . On Easter-Monday, 1725. In which Mr. Lock's Notions of Personality and Identity are confuted* (2d ed., London, 1725), signature A².

10. Irvin Ehrenpreis, "The Meaning of Gulliver's Last Voyage," in *Swift: A Collection of Critical Essays*, ed. Ernest Lee Tuveson (Englewood Cliffs, N. J.: Prentice-Hall, 1964), pp. 136–37. Also see Isaac Watts, *Philosophical Essays on Various Subjects . . . with Some Remarks on Mr. Locke's Essay on the Human Understanding* (London, 1733), in *The Works*, ed. George Burder, 6 vols. (London, 1810–1811), 5:576; Bayle's *Dictionnaire Historique et Critique*, 4 vols. (4th ed., Amsterdam, 1730), 2:288; and the *Dictionary Historical and Critical*, 5 vols. (2d ed., London, 1734–1738), 2:661–62.

11. The quotation from Pope is in Joseph Spence, *Observations, Anecdotes, and Characters of Books and Men*, ed. James M. Osborn, 2 vols. (Oxford: Clarendon Press, 1966), 1:92, no. 212.

12. Matthew Prior, *A Dialogue Between Mr: John Lock and Seigneur de*

Montaigne, in his *Literary Works*, ed. H. B. Wright and M. K. Spears, 2 vols. (Oxford: Clarendon Press, 1971), 1:620–22, 624–25. For the tradition of this work, the Lucianic dialogue, see Frederick M. Keener, *English Dialogues of the Dead: A Critical History* (New York: Columbia University Press, 1973).

13. Spence, *Anecdotes*, 1:92, no. 212.

14. Alexander Pope, *The Twickenham Edition of the Works of Alexander Pope*, ed. John Butt, 11 vols. (London: Methuen, 1939–1969), vol. 4, *Imitations of Horace*, ed. John Butt (2d ed., 1953), p. 281, lines 25–26.

15. Spence, *Anecdotes*, 1:217, no. 510; and Locke, *Essay* 2.1.4. For the new concern with thinking about thinking, see especially John W. Yolton, *Perceptual Acquaintance from Descartes to Reid* (Minneapolis: University of Minnesota Press, 1984); and James G. Buickerood, "The Natural History of the Understanding: Locke and the Rise of Facultative Logic in the Eighteenth Century," *History and Philosophy of Logic* 6 (1985): 157–90.

16. Richard Burthogge, *An Essay Upon Reason and the Nature of Spirits* (London, 1694), p. 4.

17. R. A. Sayce, *The Essays of Montaigne: A Critical Exploration* (Evanston, Ill.: Northwestern University Press, 1972), p. 107.

18. *The Essays of Michael Seigneur de Montaigne*, trans. Charles Cotton, 3 vols. (3d ed., London, 1700), 1:415.

19. Richard L. Regosin, *The Matter of My Book: Montaigne's Essais as the Book of the Self* (Berkeley and Los Angeles: University of California Press, 1977), pp. 24–25.

20. Samuel Taylor Coleridge, *The Philosophical Lectures*, ed. Kathleen Coburn (London: Pilot Press, 1949), pp. 379, 381.

21. Thomas Hearne, *Remarks and Collections*, ed. C. E. Doble et al., 11 vols. (Oxford: Oxford Historical Society, Clarendon Press, 1885–1921), 11:395.

22. George Berkeley, *The Works of George Berkeley, Bishop of Cloyne*, ed. A. A. Luce and T. E. Jessop, 9 vols. (London: Nelson, 1948–1957), 1:86, no. 700.

23. Samuel Bold, *Some Considerations on the Principle Objections And Arguments which have been Publish'd against Mr. Lock's Essay of Humane Understanding* (London, 1699), pp. 1–2.

24. Sir Samuel Garth, *The Dispensary*, in *Poems on Affairs of State: Augustan Satirical Verse, 1660–1714*, ed. George de F. Lord, 7 vols. (New Haven: Yale University Press, 1963–1975), vol. 6, ed. Frank H. Ellis (1970), p. 116.

25. *A Free but Modest Censure On the late Controversial Writings and Debates of The Lord Bishop of Worcester and Mr. Locke* (London, 1698), pp. 5–6, 10. The same author also accuses Locke of pedantry, in that he contradicts *"establish'd Opinions upon very slight grounds"* and *"spins Volumes ... barely out of his own Thoughts"* (p. 9). For some other contemporary defenses of Stillingfleet against Locke, see, for example, *The History of the Works of the Learned* 2 (January 1700): 41; and Winch Holdsworth, *A Defence of the Doctrine of the Resurrection of the Same Body ... in which the Character, Writings, and Religious Principles of Mr. Lock ... are Distinctly considered* (London, 1727), part 1, pp. 85–111.

26. Richard C. Boys notes Locke's praise of *King Arthur* and his letter to Molyneux on 11 September 1697: "sir R. B.'s vein in poetry be what every body must allow him to have an extraordinary talent in." See *Sir Richard Blackmore and the Wits* (1949; reprint ed., New York: Octagon Books, 1969), p. 28. Also see *The Correspondence of John Locke*, ed. E. S. DeBeer, 8 vols. (Oxford: Clarendon Press, 1976), 6:190.

27. Sir Richard Blackmore, *A Satyr Against Wit*, in *Poems On Affairs of State*, 6:139–40.

28. Jonathan Swift, *Remarks upon a Book, Intitled, The Rights of the Christian Church*, in *The Prose Works of Jonathan Swift*, ed. Herbert Davis, 14 vols. (Oxford: Basil Blackwell, 1938–1968), 2:79–80. The association of Locke with the Deists was not one he openly relished. See Locke's letter to Molyneux (15 June 1697) and Molyneux's reply (20 July 1697) in Locke's *Correspondence*, 6:143–44, 163–64.

29. Hume, *Treatise*, p. 259.

30. [James Carkesse], *Lucida Intervalla: Containing divers Miscellaneous Poems, Written at Finsbury and Bethlem by the Doctors Patient Extraordinary* (1679; reprint ed., Los Angeles: William Andrews Clark Memorial Library, Augustan Reprint Society Nos. 195–96, 1979), pp. 5, 8. Also see Michael V. DePorte's introduction to this edition (pp. iii–xi).

31. Michael V. DePorte, "Vehicles of Delusion: Swift, Locke, and the Madhouse Poems of James Carkesse," in *Psychology and Literature in the Eighteenth Century*, ed. Christopher Fox (New York: AMS Studies in the Eighteenth Century, 1987), pp. 69–86; esp. 79.

32. See Christopher Fox, "The Myth of Narcissus in Swift's *Travels*," *Eighteenth-Century Studies* 20 (1986–1987): 17–33, esp. 30–31n.

33. Ehrenpreis, "The Meaning of Gulliver's Last Voyage," pp. 134–37; and Rosalie L. Colie, "Gulliver, the Locke-Stillingfleet Controversy, and the Nature of Man," *History of Ideas News Letter* 2 (1956):

58–62. In his "Man, Horse and Drill: Temple's *Essay on Popular Discontents* and Gulliver's Fourth Voyage" (*English Studies* 55 [1974]: 358–60), Clive T. Probyn has also noted a connection between Locke-Stillingfleet and *Gulliver's Travels*. A more recent attempt to connect *Gulliver* and Locke's theory is less convincing. See Spencer Wertz and Linda Wertz, "Some Correlations Between Swift's Gulliver and Locke on Personal Identity," *Journal of Thought* 10 (1975): 262–70.

34. Jonathan Swift, *Gulliver's Travels*, in the *Prose Works*, 11:236. Compare Isaac Watts's remark a few years later: "Doth not this author allow, in Section 19, that if Socrates asleep puts forth any actions, and is not conscious of it when he awakes, sleeping and waking Socrates is not the same person? And are they not two persons according to his notion?" (*Philosophical Essays*, in *The Works*, 5:626.)

5. OF CONTROVERSY AND CONVIVIALITY, AND A PEDANT'S PROGRESS

1. William Cowper, as quoted in Alexander Pope et al., *The Memoirs of the Extraordinary Life, Works, and Discoveries of Martinus Scriblerus*, ed. Charles Kerby-Miller (1950; reprint ed., New York: Russell and Russell, 1966), p. vii. All further references to *The Memoirs* are to this edition, cited in the text by page number only. For details about the formation of the Scriblerus Club, see Kerby-Miller's introduction to the work (pp. 1–77).

2. Martin Price, *To the Palace of Wisdom: Studies in Order and Energy from Dryden to Blake* (1964; reprint ed., Carbondale: Southern Illinois University Press, 1970), p. 216.

3. For commentary on the Scriblerus papers and project, see Robert T. Allen, *The Clubs of Augustan London* (Cambridge, Mass.: Harvard University Press, 1933), pp. 260–83; Robert A. Erickson, "Situations of Identity in the *Memoirs of Martinus Scriblerus*," *Modern Language Quarterly* 26 (1965): 388–400; Irvin Ehrenpreis, *Swift: The Man, His Works, and the Age*, 3 vols. (Cambridge, Mass.: Harvard University Press, 1962–1983), 2:722–27; Joseph M. Levine, *Dr. Woodward's Shield: History, Science, and Satire in Augustan England* (Berkeley and Los Angeles: University of California Press, 1977), pp. 238–52; Hopewell Selby, "'Never Finding Repast': Satire and Self-Extension in the Early Eighteenth Century," in *Probability, Time, and Space in Eighteenth-Century Literature*, ed. Paula R. Backscheider (New York: AMS Studies in the Eighteenth Century, 1979), pp. 217–48; Robert

C. Steensma, *John Arbuthnot* (New York: Twayne, 1979), pp. 68–92; Reginald Berry, "Absurder Projects: Scriblerus, Chaucer, and the Discommodities of Marriage," *English Studies in Canada* 7 (1981): 141–55; C. J. Rawson and F. P. Lock, "Scriblerian Epigrams by Thomas Parnell," *Review of English Studies* 33 (1982): 148–57; and Roger D. Lund, "Res et Verba: Scriblerian Satire and the Fate of Language," *Bucknell Review* 27 (1983): 63–80.

4. Northrop Frye, *The Anatomy of Criticism* (Princeton: Princeton University Press, 1957), esp. pp. 308–12. For helpful information on the Menippean tradition, and some qualifications of Frye's account, see Bud Korkowski, "Genre and Satiric Strategy in Burton's *Anatomy of Melancholy,*" *Genre* 8 (1975): 174–87; Eugene P. Kirk, *Menippean Satire: An Annotated Catalogue of Texts and Criticism* (New York: Garland Publishing, 1980); and James F. Woodruff, "*Rasselas* and the Traditions of 'Menippean Satire,'" in *Samuel Johnson: New Critical Essays*, ed. Isobel Grundy (London: Vision Press, 1984), pp. 158–85.

5. Joseph Spence, *Observations, Anecdotes, and Characters of Books and Men*, ed. James M. Osborn, 2 vols. (Oxford: Clarendon Press, 1966), 1:56, no. 135.

6. Athenaeus, *The Deipnosophists*, trans. Charles B. Gulick, Loeb Classical Library, 7 vols. (London, 1927), 1:3, 9, 5. All further references are to this translation, cited in the text by volume and page number (e.g., 2:229).

7. C. A. Van Rooy, *Studies in Classical Satire and Related Literary Theory* (Leiden: E. J. Brill, 1966), p. 5.

8. Frye, *Anatomy*, p. 311.

9. Athenaeus, *Deipnosophists*, ed. Gulick, 1:xiii.

10. *The Memoirs*, ed. Kerby-Miller, p. 27, and the "Rhymed Invitations to Scriblerus Meetings and Replies," Appendix I, pp. 351–59. For the survival of the "deipnosophical" tradition in eighteenth-century Europe, see Ernst Robert Curtius, *European Literature and the Latin Middle Ages*, trans. Willard R. Trask (New York: Harper and Row, 1963), pp. 58–59. William King has one of his characters tell another that no one "can be a Scholar without being an expert in the whole method of Athenaeus's Cookery. What quarrels, Madam, do you think there have been between grave and learned men, about spelling a Greek word.... Pray read Athenaeus, Madam; and you will be convinced of it." (*The Original Works of William King*, 3 vols. [London, 1776], 1:160.)

11. *The Twickenham Edition of the Works of Alexander Pope*, ed. John Butt, 11 vols. (New Haven: Yale University Press, 1939–1969), vol. 4, *Imitations of Horace*, ed. John Butt (2d ed., 1953), p. 17, line 128.

12. Ehrenpreis, *Swift*, 2:725.

13. *The Memoirs*, ed. Kerby-Miller, p. 31.

14. Price, *Palace of Wisdom*, p. 217.

15. Kenneth Maclean, *John Locke and English Literature of the Eighteenth Century* (New Haven: Yale University Press, 1936), pp. 10–11.

16. Paul Oskar Kristeller, *Renaissance Thought: The Classic, Scholastic, and Humanist Strains* (New York: Harper and Row, 1961), p. 12.

17. The quotation is taken from *A Free but Modest Censure On the Late Controversial Writings and Debates of The Lord Bishop of Worcester and Mr. Locke* (London, 1698), p. 3. For an eloquent early defense of controversy itself, see Meric Casaubon's *A Letter . . . to Peter du Moulin* (Cambridge, England, 1669), esp. p. 18. Later ones include William Wotton's *Reflections Upon Ancient and Modern Learning* (London, 1694), p. 343; and "An Apology for the Use of certain Terms in controversial Writings, which some think harsh and indecent," *Present State of the Republick of Letters* 11 (March 1733): 202–12. The 1733 author argues that, against "the Adversaries of Reveal'd Religion," no language is too harsh; in fact, crude language and name-calling "may be employ'd without the least Violation of good Manners" or even "Christian Vertue" (202). The editor of the *Present State* replies, "We have inserted this Letter as it came to our Hands; but, as we have no Inclination to engage in a Dispute on this subject, we hope to be excused [from] giving any Judgment on it" (212). Though there is some work on the discourse of dispute, more needs to be done, especially on the eighteenth-century discussion of *controversy* and its connections with, for instance, the concept of satire itself. One starting point might be provided by the special issue of *Prose Studies* (vol. 9, September 1986) edited by Thomas N. Corns and titled *The Literature of Controversy: Polemical Strategy from Milton to Junius*.

18. Sir William Temple, "Some Thoughts upon Reviewing the *Essay of Ancient and Modern Learning*," in *Five Miscellaneous Essays*, ed. Samuel Holt Monk (Ann Arbor: University of Michigan Press, 1963), p. 89; John Locke, *The Educational Writings*, ed. James L. Axtell (Cambridge, England: Cambridge University Press, 1968), p. 200; and Joseph Addison and Richard Steele, *The Spectator*, ed. D. F. Bond, 5 vols. (Oxford: Clarendon Press, 1965), 2:429.

19. *The Original Works of William King*, 1 : 160.

20. *A Miscellany of the Wits*, ed. K. N. Colville (London: Allan, 1920), p. 281. Compare this with Locke's comment in *An Essay Concerning Human Understanding*: "Men would give off a wrong Argument... if in their Disputes they proposed to themselves the finding and imbracing [*sic*] of Truth, and not a Contest for Victory" (4.7.11).

21. Jonathan Swift, *Prose Works*, ed. Herbert Davis, 14 vols. (Oxford: Basil Blackwell, 1938–1968), 9 : 166; Pope, *Twickenham Edition*, vol. 5, *The Dunciad*, ed. James Sutherland (3d ed., 1963), p. 369, line 255n; *The Correspondence of Alexander Pope*, ed. George Sherburn, 5 vols. (Oxford: Clarendon Press, 1956), 1 : 493; and John Arbuthnot, *A Brief Account of Mr. John Ginglicutt's Treatise Concerning the Altercation Or Scolding Of the Ancients*, in *The Life and Works of John Arbuthnot*, ed. George Aitken (1892; reprint ed., New York: Russell and Russell, 1968), pp. 383, 391.

22. Anthony, Earl of Shaftesbury, *Characteristics of Men, Manners, Opinions, Times*, ed. J. M. Robertson, 2 vols. (1900; reprint ed., Gloucester, Mass.: Peter Smith, 1963), 1 : 99.

23. It should also be noted that though the Scriblerians, like Locke before them, continually stated their dislike for controversy, they were often involved in it. Throughout his work Locke also disdains disputing. But the Locke-Stillingfleet controversy is longer than the *Essay Concerning Human Understanding* itself.

24. John Webster, *Academiarum Examen, or the Examination of Academies* (London, 1654), p. 38; and Pope, *The Dunciad*, pp. 360–61, lines 189–92, 195–98. The issues in the debate between humanist and schoolman in Pope's lifetime are discussed by Aubrey L. Williams in *Pope's Dunciad: A Study of Its Meaning* (1955; reprint ed., Camden, N. J.: Archon, 1968).

25. *The Poems of Jonathan Swift*, ed. Sir Harold Williams, 3 vols. (Oxford: Clarendon Press, 1958), 3 : 900.

26. Jonathan Swift, *A Tale of a Tub*, ed. A. C. Guthkelch and D. Nichol Smith (2d ed., Oxford: Clarendon Press, 1958), p. 85.

27. Parnell and Swift had been trained in the scholastic system at Trinity College, Dublin, and Arbuthnot at Oxford. For Swift's response to "strict syllogistic disputations," see Irvin Ehrenpreis's informative chapters on "Trinity College" and Swift's "Studies" in *Swift*, 1: esp. 58ff.

28. Joseph Glanvill, *The Vanity of Dogmatizing* (1661; reprint ed., Sussex-Hove: Harvester Press, 1970), p. 152.

29. Joseph Levine points to this ambivalence when he tells us that "the Aristotle of the schoolmen was called into question and found wanting, even though Aristotle continued to furnish much of the basic material of the university and the training of the theologians." ("Ancients and Moderns Reconsidered," *Eighteenth-Century Studies* 15 [Fall 1981–1982]: 81.)

30. John Locke, *Mr. Locke's Reply to the Right Reverend the Lord Bishop of Worcester's Letter* (London, 1697), pp. 162–63.

31. Richard Aaron notes this ambivalence, for instance, in Locke's careful use of the word *substance*: "He finds it difficult to justify [the] use of the concept, and yet," with the notable exception of his theory of *personal* identity, "he cannot proceed without it." (*John Locke* [3d ed., Oxford: Clarendon Press, 1971], p. 142.)

32. James Gibson, *Locke's Theory of Knowledge and Its Historical Relations* (Cambridge, England: Cambridge University Press, 1931), pp. 118–19.

33. See George Berkeley, *The Works of George Berkeley, Bishop of Cloyne*, ed. A. A. Luce and T. E. Jessop, 9 vols. (London: Nelson, 1948–1957), especially 1:87, no. 713; and above, pp. 45–46.

34. Swift, *Prose Works*, 2:97.

35. Swift, *Prose Works*, 2:80; and pp. 19–20 above.

36. W. B. Carnochan, *Lemuel Gulliver's Mirror for Man* (Berkeley and Los Angeles: University of California Press, 1968), p. 149. Speaking of the Scriblerians as a group, John Traugott comments that they "are universally concerned with learned bagatelle because they are not finally removed from scholastic habits of mind." And he points out of Swift in particular: "His anti-intellectualism is an obvious fact; and that the intellectual habits of scholasticism formed his mind is an equally obvious fact." (*Tristram Shandy's World* [Berkeley and Los Angeles: University of California Press, 1954], p. 17.) More recently, Clive Probyn has similarly argued that the "cultural world of Swift had clearly digested the terms and methods of traditional Aristotelian logic and had assimilated its elements into [a] world picture." ("Swift and the Human Predicament," in *The Art of Jonathan Swift*, ed. Clive Probyn [London: Vision Press, 1978], p. 60.) Both comments are, on the whole, just.

37. Dugald Stewart, *The Collected Works of Dugald Stewart*, ed. Sir William Hamilton, 11 vols. (Edinburgh, 1854), 1:604.

6. "A MASTER-PIECE" FOR "NONE BUT A PHILOSOPHER"

1. Kerby-Miller finds it safe to make this attribution (*Memoirs*, pp. 295–96).

2. John Kersey, *Dictionarium Anglo-Britannicum* (1708; reprint ed., Menston, England: Scolar Press, 1969), s.v. "subsistence."

3. Kerby-Miller also notes the Clarke-Collins parody. He tends to dismiss the importance of the debate itself, which he sees as "interesting less for its philosophical importance than as an illustration of the intellectual interests and temper of the time." He also misses the controversiality of Locke's theory and its key place in Collins's arguments; and he does not discuss the last two pamphlets of the dispute, where personal identity emerges as a central issue. Despite this, his notes are helpful and should be consulted. That eighteenth-century readers recognized the parody is suggested by Warton's comment, decades after the dispute: "This whole chapter is an inimitable ridicule on Collins's arguments against Clarke." (*The Works of Alexander Pope*, ed. W. Elwin and W. J. Courthope, 10 vols. [1871–1889; reprint ed., New York: Gordian Press, 1967], 10:332n.) Also see *The Memoirs*, pp. 281–85.

4. Edward Stillingfleet, *The Bishop of Worcester's Answer to Mr. Locke's Second Letter, Wherein his Notion of Ideas Is prov'd to be Inconsistent with it self And with the Articles of the Christian Faith* (London, 1698), pp. 35–36.

5. [Andrew Baxter], *An Enquiry into the Nature of the Human Soul; Wherein the Immateriality of the Soul is evinced from the Principles of Reason and Philosophy* (London, ca. 1733), p. 144n.

6. Samuel Clarke, *The Works of Samuel Clarke*, 4 vols. (London, 1738), 3:722, 730.

7. Anthony Collins, in *Works of Clarke*, 3:751.

8. *Works of Clarke*, 3:844, 902.

9. David Hume, *A Treatise of Human Nature*, ed. L. A. Selby-Bigge, rev. P. H. Nidditch (2d ed., Oxford: Clarendon Press, 1978), p. 261. Since *The Memoirs* remained unpublished until 1741, there is very little possibility that Hume would have seen this chapter, even though it dates back to 1714.

10. Henry Lee, *Anti-Scepticism: Or, Notes upon each Chapter of Mr. Lock's Essay concerning Humane Understanding* (London, 1702), p. 125.

11. Anthony Collins, in *Works of Clarke*, 3:878, 876, 870.

12. John Sergeant, *Solid Philosophy Asserted, Against the Fancies of the Ideists.... With Reflexions on Mr. Locke's Essay Concerning Human Understanding* (London, 1697), p. 263.

13. *Works of Clarke*, 3:844–45, 851–52, 902, 904.

14. Leslie Fiedler, *Freaks: Myths and Images of the Secret Self* (New York: Simon and Schuster, 1978), pp. 206–7.

15. That the same man can be different persons does not seem strange to us, accustomed as we are to pleas of temporary insanity and the like. But this conclusion disturbed some in Locke's age, who believed with Henry Lee that if *"Consciousness* only makes a Person the same, and the want of it a *different* Person, then no Courts of *Humane* Judicature can be justly establish'd." (*Anti-Scepticism*, p. 127.) For some current speculations on identity and law, see John Brydall, *Non Compos Mentis* (London, 1700).

EPILOGUE

1. Cuthbert Comment [Abraham Tucker], *Man in quest of Himself: Or A Defence of the Individuality of the Human Mind, or Self* (1763), in *Metaphysical Tracts by English Philosophers of the Eighteenth Century*, ed. Samuel Parr (London: Edward Lumley, 1837), p. 173.

2. Laurence Sterne, *Tristram Shandy*, ed. James A. Work (New York: Odyssey Press, 1940), p. 525.

3. Philip Doddridge, *A Course of Lectures on the Principal Subjects in Pneumatology, Ethics, and Divinity* (London, 1763), p. 41. Doddridge died in 1751.

4. George Gordon, Lord Byron, *Don Juan*, in *Byron*, ed. Jerome J. McGann (Oxford: Oxford University Press, 1986), p. 373.

5. See, for instance, Douglas Lane Patey, "Art and Integrity: Concepts of Self in Alexander Pope and Edward Young," *Modern Philology* 83 (1986): 364–78.

6. John Sitter, "The Argument of Pope's *Epistle to Cobham*," *Studies in English Literature* 17 (1977): 448. Also see Leopold Damrosch's chapter on "Psychology" in *The Imaginative World of Alexander Pope* (Berkeley and Los Angeles: University of California Press, 1987), pp. 139–59.

7. Georges Poulet, *Studies in Human Time*, trans. Elliot Coleman (Baltimore: Johns Hopkins University Press, 1956), p. 23.

8. Edward Stillingfleet, *The Bishop of Worcester's Answer to Mr. Locke's Second Letter, Wherein his Notion of Ideas Is prov'd to be Inconsistent*

with it self And with the Articles of the Christian Faith (London, 1698), p. 59; and David Hume, *A Treatise of Human Nature*, ed. L. A. Selby-Bigge, rev. P. H. Nidditch (2d ed., Oxford: Clarendon Press, 1978), p. 635.

9. Compare Locke's chapter *"Of our Complex Ideas of Substances"* (*Essay* 2.23.12) with Epistle 1, lines 189–204, of *An Essay on Man*, which includes the couplet: "Why has not Man a microscopic eye? / For this plain reason, Man is not a Fly." See *The Twickenham Edition of the Works of Alexander Pope*, ed. John Butt, 11 vols. (New Haven: Yale University Press, 1939–1969), vol. 3, part 1, *An Essay on Man*, ed. Maynard Mack (1950), pp. 38–40.

10. John Locke, *A Letter to the Right Reverend Edward Ld Bishop of Worcester concerning some Passages relating to Mr. Locke's Essay of Humane Understanding: In a late Discourse of his Lordships, in Vindication of the Trinity* (London, 1697), p. 40. In the same pamphlet (p. 58), Locke goes on to tell Stillingfleet that "by the Existence of *Thought* in me, to which *something* that thinks is evidently and necessarily connected in my Mind, I come to be certain that there exists in me *something* that thinks, though of that *something* which I call *Substance* also, I have but a very obscure, confused Idea."

11. Peter Browne, *The Procedure, Extent, and Limits of the Human Understanding* (2d ed., London, 1729), pp. 73, 78–79.

12. Hume, *Treatise*, p. 252. For some other occurrences see, for example, Edward Stillingfleet, *Discourse in Vindication of the Doctrine of the Trinity* (London, 1696), p. 259; Samuel Clarke, *The Works of Samuel Clarke*, 4 vols. (London, 1738), 3:790–91; Anthony, Earl of Shaftesbury, *Characteristics of Men, Manners, Opinions, Times*, ed. J. M. Robertson, 2 vols. (1900; reprint ed., Gloucester, Mass.: Peter Smith, 1963), 2:275; and [Andrew Baxter], *An Enquiry into the Nature of the Human Soul; Wherein the Immateriality of the Soul is evinced from the Principles of Reason and Philosophy* (London, ca. 1733), p. 144n.

13. Pope, *The Twickenham Edition*, vol. 3, part 2, *Epistles to Several Persons*, ed. F. W. Bateson (2d ed., 1961), p. 18, lines 49–50 (my italics). All further *Cobham* citations are to this edition, cited in the text by line numbers alone.

14. Thomas Reid, *Essays on the Intellectual Powers of Man* (1785; reprint ed., New York: Garland Publishing, 1971), p. 336.

15. George Berkeley, *The Works of George Berkeley, Bishop of Cloyne*, ed. A. A. Luce and T. E. Jessop, 9 vols. (London: Nelson, 1948–1957), 2:233.

16. *Works of Clarke*, 3:844.

17. On this point, see Christopher Fox, "'Gone as soon as Found': Pope's *Epistle to Cobham* and the Death-day as Moment of Truth," *Studies in English Literature* 20 (1980): 431–48.

18. Hume, *Treatise*, pp. 120, 253, 419–20; and Pope, *The Twickenham Edition*, vol. 3, part 1, *An Essay on Man*, Epistle 2, p. 71, line 132. "As a peg for hanging anecdotes on no doubt Pope's hypothesis" of a ruling passion "was adequate," writes Bateson, in the standard edition. See Pope, *Twickenham*, vol. 3, part 2, *Epistles*, ed. Bateson, p. xxxv.

19. Melinda Alliker Rabb, "Lost in a House of Mirrors: Pope's *Imitations of Horace*," *Papers on Language and Literature* 18 (1982): 302.

20. *The Twickenham Edition*, vol. 4, *Imitations of Horace*, ed. John Butt (2d ed., 1953), pp. 291–93, lines 163–70, 174–75.

21. Hume, *Treatise*, p. 252.

22. See Vincent Perronet, *A Second Vindication of Mr. Locke, Wherein his Sentiments relating to Personal Identity are clear'd from some Mistakes of the Rev. Dr. Butler, in his Dissertation on that Subject* (London, 1738).

23. [Samuel Johnson], *Elementa Philosophica: containing chiefly Noetica, Or Things relating to the Mind or Understanding: And Ethica, Or Things relating to Ethical Behaviour* (Philadelphia, 1752), pp. 39–40.

24. See Roger Kenneth French, *Robert Whytt, the Soul, and Medicine* (London: Wellcome Institute for the History of Medicine, 1969), esp. p. 144.

25. Henry Lee, *Anti-Scepticism: Or, Notes upon each Chapter of Mr. Lock's Essay concerning Humane Understanding* (London, 1702), p. 130.

26. Ian Watt, *The Rise of the Novel* (Berkeley and Los Angeles: University of California Press, 1957), p. 192.

27. James Boswell, entry for 29 July 1769, in *Boswell in Search of a Wife, 1766–1769*, ed. Frank Brady and F. A. Pottle (New York: McGraw-Hill, 1957), p. 258.

28. James Boswell, entry for 13 May 1763, in *The London Journal, 1762–1763*, ed. F. A. Pottle (New York: McGraw-Hill, 1950), p. 258 (my italics).

29. John N. Morris, *Versions of the Self: Studies in English Autobiography from John Bunyan to John Stuart Mill* (New York: Basic Books, 1966), p. 193.

30. James Boswell, entry for 13 January 1776, in *The Ominous Years, 1774–1776*, ed. Charles Ryskamp and F. A. Pottle (New York: McGraw-Hill, 1963), p. 220.

31. Stephen D. Cox, "*The Stranger Within Thee*": *Concepts of the Self in Late-Eighteenth-Century Literature* (Pittsburgh: University of Pittsburgh

Press, 1980), p. 7. On the later period, one might also see J. O. Lyons, *The Invention of the Self* (Carbondale: Southern Illinois University Press, 1978); Ann Hartle, *The Modern Self in Rousseau's "Confessions": A Reply to St. Augustine* (Notre Dame, Ind.: University of Notre Dame Press, 1984); and Patricia Meyer Spacks, *Imagining a Self: Autobiography and Novel in Eighteenth-Century England* (Cambridge, Mass.: Harvard University Press, 1976).

32. Fredric V. Bogel, "Structure and Substantiality in Later Eighteenth-Century Literature," *Studies in Burke and His Time* 15 (1973–1974): 143–45. Also see Bogel's *Literature and Insubstantiality in Later Eighteenth-Century England* (Princeton: Princeton University Press, 1984).

33. [Edmund Law], *A Defence of Mr. Locke's Opinion concerning Personal Identity* (1769), in *The Works of John Locke*, 10 vols. (1823; reprint ed., Darmstadt: Scientia Verlag, 1963), 3:192.

34. Edward Young, *Conjectures on Original Composition* (1759; reprint ed., Menston, England: Scolar Press, 1966), pp. 52–53.

35. William Cowper, *Poems*, ed. H. I. Fausset (London: Everyman Library, 1930), p. 371, lines 284–85. For a related consideration, see Jean H. Hagstrum, "Towards a Profile of the Word *Conscious* in Eighteenth-Century Literature," in *Psychology and Literature in the Eighteenth Century*, ed. Christopher Fox (New York: AMS Studies in the Eighteenth Century, 1987), pp. 23–50.

36. Marshall Brown, "The Pre-Romantic Discovery of Consciousness," *Studies in Romanticism* 17 (1978): 398–99.

37. [Thomas Burnet], *Remarks upon An Essay Concerning Humane Understanding. In A Letter Address'd To the Author* (London, 1697), p. 9. Also see Burnet's *Second Remarks upon an Essay Concerning Humane Understanding* (London, 1697), pp. 16–17.

38. For some comments on how later writers come up with "a reinstatement of something strangely like the mysterious underlying substance...of the older Schools," see Clement C. J. Webb, *God and Personality* (London: George Allen and Unwin, 1918), pp. 58–59.

Index

Aaron, Richard, 156n.31

Addison, Joseph, 89. See also *The Spectator*

Alciphron: Or, the Minute Philosopher (Berkeley), 2, 45, 62–63

Allen, Robert T., 152n.3

Allison, Henry E., 17, 29, 30

Amnesia, 37, 61

Anatomy of Melancholy (Burton), 83

Animal spirits, 144–45n.25

An Answer to Mr. Clarke's Third Defence. See Collins, Anthony

Anti-Scepticism: Or, Notes upon each Chapter of Mr. Lock's Essay Concerning Humane Understanding. See Lee, Henry

"The Apology for Raymond Sebond" (Montaigne), 73–74

Aquinas, Saint Thomas, 60; *Summa*, 22

Arbuthnot, John, 19, 20, 57, 69, 92, 95, 96, 137n.27, 155n.27; *A Brief Account of John Ginglicutt's Treatise Concerning the Altercation or Scolding of the Ancients*, 90. See also *Memoirs of . . . Scriblerus*; Scriblerians

Aristotle, 92, 94

Aristotle's Masterpiece, 67, 148n.50

Ashe, St. George, 27, 139n.2

Athenaeus of Naucratis, 83–85, 153n.10; *The Deipnosophists*, 83–84, 85

Augustine, Saint, 21–22

Balz, Alfred G. A., 135–36n.14

Bateson, F. W., 125, 160n.18

Baxter, Andrew, 159n.12; *Enquiry into the Nature of the Human Soul*, 102

Bayle, Pierre, 13, 149n.10; *Dictionnaire Historique et Critique*, 71

Beattie, James, 132n.4

Behan, David P., 33, 142nn. 14 and 16

Bentley, Richard, 41, 82

Berkeley, George, 38; and consciousness, 62–63, 123; on Locke's theory of personal identity, 45–46, 62–63, 64; and scholasticism, 92–93; and Stillingfleet, 45, 74; and the substantial self, 45–46, 98
—works: *Alciphron: Or, the Minute Philosopher*, 2, 45, 62–63; correspondence, 19, 137n.27; Notebooks, 45; *The Principles of Human Knowledge*, 19, 45, 93; *Three Dialogues Between Hylas and Philonous*, 45, 46, 123

Berry, Reginald, 152–53n.3

Bibliotheque Raisonnée des Ouvrages des Savans de l'Europe, 134n.10

Blackmore, Sir Richard, 75; *A Satyr Against Wit*, 76

Bodily identity, 22, 140n.3

Boethius, 15; *Treatise against Eutyches and Nestorius*, 15, 21

Bogel, Fredric V., 129

Bold, Samuel, 75, 139n.38

Bolingbroke, Henry St. John, Viscount, 126, 141n.11

Boswell, James, 127–29; *Boswell in Search of a Wife*, 127; *Life of Johnson*, 147n.45; *The London Journal*, 128; *The Ominous Years*, 128

Boyle, Robert: *Some Physico-Theological Considerations about the Possibility of the Resurrection*, 22

Boyle Lectures, 48, 57

Boys, Richard C., 151n.26

Brain, 50, 105

Braudy, Leo, 9

A Brief Account of John Ginglicutt's Treatise Concerning the Altercation or Scolding of the Ancients (Arbuthnot), 90

The British Apollo, 38, 68, 96, 110

Brown, Marshall, 130

Brown, S. C., 144n.16

Browne, Peter, 38, 45, 122; *Procedure, Extent, and Limits of the Human Understanding*, 122. *See also* Perronet-Browne debate

Brydall, John, 158n.15

Budgell, Eustace, 66

Buickerood, James G., 133n.7, 150n.15

Burnet, Thomas, 38, 149n.8, 161n.37; *Remarks upon An Essay Concerning Humane Understanding*, 39, 130

Burthogge, Richard, 38, 67, 141–

42n.13; *An Essay Upon Reason and the Nature of Spirits*, 73

Burton, Robert: *Anatomy of Melancholy*, 83

Butler, Joseph, 9; on consciousness, 10, 56, 64, 127; on Locke's theory of personal identity, 2, 10, 11, 14, 17–18, 45–46, 55–57, 59, 127; and moral accountability, 56; and substantial self, 11, 56; "Of Personal Identity," 2, 10, 46, 56, 57. *See also* Butler-Perronet debate

Butler-Perronet debate, 33, 62, 77, 146n.31

Byron, George Gordon, Lord: *Don Juan*, 120

Cannibalism, and personal identity, 22, 60

Carkesse, James: *Lucida Intervalla*, 77–78

Carnochan, W. B., 94, 137–38n.25

Carroll, R. T., 144n.8

Casaubon, Meric, 154n.17

Cassirer, Ernst, 8

Cena, the, 83

Chambers, Ephraim, 38, 57, 58–59; *The Cyclopaedia: Or, An Universal Dictionary of Arts and Sciences*, 38, 58–59

Christ Church wits, 83

Christianity Not Mysterious (Toland), 41

Christian Mortalism, 49, 145n.27

Cicero, 12, 89

Clarke, Samuel, 38, 101, 105–6; and consciousness, 49, 50, 51, 53, 123; and Samuel Johnson, 69, 148n.4; and moral accountability, 16, 52, 54–55, 108; pamphlets against Collins, 7, 16, 19, 49, 50, 51, 52, 54, 55, 61, 62, 104, 108, 123, 145n.26, 159n.12; on Resurrection,

52, 54–55, 108; and soul, 49. *See also* Clarke-Collins controversy

Clarke-Collins controversy, 7, 10, 18–19, 21, 48–56, 61–62, 69, 70, 77, 82, 101–2, 103, 123, 145n.26, 157n.3. *See also* Clarke, Samuel; Collins, Anthony; Maxwell, John

Clarke-Leibniz controversy, 149n.5

Clendon, John: *Tractatus . . . de Persona. Or, A Treatise of the Word Person*, 15

Cockburn, Catherine Trotter. *See* Trotter, Catherine

Cogito, the, 16–17, 140n.6

Coleridge, Samuel Taylor, 120; *The Philosophical Lectures*, 74

Colic, Rosalie L., 78, 94, 137n.29

Collingwood, R. G., 136n.15

Collins, Anthony, 38, 125; and consciousness, 18–19, 53, 55; *Discourse on Free Thinking*, 48; and Locke, 48; and Locke's theory of personal identity, 50, 52–54, 55, 106–8; pamphlets against Clarke, 18–19, 49, 50, 52–54, 56, 61, 104, 106; and self, 52–53; and the soul, 49. *See also* Clarke-Collins controversy

Concern, 33, 35

Conscience, and consciousness, 12–14

Conscientia: in Cicero, 12; and consciousness, 136n.14

Consciousness, 10, 11, 33, 121; alienation of, 35–37, 60–64; and Berkeley, 62–63, 123; and Boswell, 127–28; and Burthogge, 73; Butler on, 10, 56, 127; Clarke on, 49, 50, 51, 53, 123; Collins on, 18–19, 53, 55; and concern, 33, 35; confused with memory, 32–33, 39, 57, 64; and *conscience*, 12–14; and *conviction*, 12–13; in Cowper, 129–30, 161n.35; critique of, 46–59, 71–

73, 101, 106–7; defined, 32–33, 44; deluded, 63; and Descartes, 135–36n.14; and drunkenness, 65; and Hume, 59; and insanity, 77–78; and law, 48; and Nathaniel Lee, 44, 48; and Locke's theory of personal identity, 12, 13–14, 17, 18, 19, 32–33, 34–37, 38, 46, 73, 106–7, 123, 134n.11, 135–36n.14; and Malebranche, 134–35n.12; in medical and physiological writings, 127; and moral accountability, 37, 64; as a new term, 11–14, 120–21, 127; and Pope, 72–73, 123–25; presupposes substance, 45, 46; problem of defining, 32–33, 49; problems translating, 12, 13; Thomas Reid on, 10, 47; responses to, 39, 46–59; and Resurrection, 37, 43, 70; and river metaphor, 47, 51, 123–24; Scriblerians on, 103–9; and *sentiment*, 12–13; and Siamese twins, 68; as synonym for soul, 127; transfer of, 35–36. *See also* Butler-Perronet debate; Clarke-Collins controversy; Locke's theory of personal identity; Locke-Stillingfleet controversy; *Memoirs of . . . Scriblerus*

Controversy, and search for truth, 89–91, 155n.20, 155n.23

Conviction, and consciousness, 12, 134n.11

Corns, Thomas N., 154n.17

Coste, Pierre, 12–13, 14, 32, 134n.11, 135n.13

Cowper, William, 81, 129–30, 161n.35; *The Task*, 129

Cox, Stephen D., 128

Cranston, Maurice, 135n.13, 138n.32

Cudworth, Ralph, 15

Curtius, Ernst Robert, 153n.10

The Cyclopaedia: Or, An Universal Dictionary of Arts and Sciences (Chambers), 38, 58–59

D'Alembert, Jean, 146n.37
Damrosch, Leopold, 158n.6
Davies, Sir John, 15
A Defence of Dr. Sherlock's Notion of a Trinity in Unity (Sherlock), 23
A Defence of Mr. Locke's Opinion concerning Personal Identity (Law), 129, 143n.1
A Defence of the Doctrine of the Resurrection of the Same Body. In . . . which the Character, Writings, and Religious Principles of Mr. Lock are Distinctly Considered (Holdsworth), 70, 139n.38, 151n.25
The Deipnosophists (Athenaeus of Naucratis), 83–84, 85
Deipnosophy, 83–88, 153n.10
Delusive identity, 77, 78
DePorte, Michael V., 77, 78, 151n.30
Descartes, René: and consciousness, 135–36n.14; *Discourse on Method*, 16; and indivisibility of thought, 17, 136–37n.23; and Locke, 28, 29, 49, 135–36n.14; *Meditations*, 17, 136–37n.23; and *Memoirs of . . . Scriblerus*, 102; and the substantial self, 16
De Trinitate (Augustine), 21–22
Dewhurst, Kenneth, 140n.5
A Dialogue Between Mr: John Lock and Seigneur de Montaigne (Prior), 69, 71–72
Dictionary Historical and Critical (Bayle), 71
Digby, Sir Kenelm, 119
Dioptrica Nova (Molyneux), 27, 139–40n.2
Discontinuity of thought. *See* Thinking, discontinuity of

A Discourse in Vindication of the Doctrine of the Trinity. See under Stillingfleet, Edward
Discourse on Free Thinking (Collins), 48
Discourse on Method (Descartes), 16
The Dispensary (Garth), 75, 76
Doctrine of the Trinity. See under Stillingfleet, Edward
Doddridge, Philip, 119
Dodwell, Henry, 49, 145n.27
Dublin Philosophical Society, 27. *See also* Molyneux, William
DuBos, Abbé, 13
Ducharme, Howard M., 146n.27
The Dunciad (Pope), 82, 90, 91, 138n.32
Dussinger, John A., 132n.1

Ehrenpreis, Irvin, 71, 78, 87, 137n.29, 140n.2, 152n.3, 155n.2
Eighteenth-Century Short Title Catalogue, and uses of *consciousness* 1700–1800, 133n.7
Empirical self, and the substantial self, 102, 121, 124–25, 127–30. *See also* Thinking, discontinuity of
Encyclopedias, 57–58
Encyclopédie, 146n.37
Epistle to Cobham. See Pope, Alexander
Erasmus of Rotterdam: *The Praise of Folly*, 82
Erickson, Robert A., 138n.33, 152n.3
Essay Concerning Human Understanding, 12, 17, 23–37 passim, 42, 46, 65–66, 73, 93, 97, 102, 107, 121, 122–23, 140n.6, 141n.9, 155n.20, 159n.10; as controversial book, 8–9, 20, 74–75, 138n.32; religious implications of, 20, 23, 41–42, 75; responses to, 3, 72; and Scriblerians, 20–21, 81–117; and the substantial self, 8, 18, 29, 30–31,

34–35, 93, 98, 102. *See also* Locke,
John
An Essay on Consciousness, 11–12, 14,
62, 133n.7; review of, 134n.10
Essays on the Intellectual Powers of Man
(Reid), 47, 123
*Essay toward a Natural History of the
Earth* (Woodward), 58
*An Essay Upon Reason and the Nature
of Spirits* (Burthogge), 73

Farquhar, George, 149n.8
Felton, Henry, 38, 45, 70–71,
139n.38
Ferguson, James, 145–46n.27
Fieldler, Leslie, 67, 109
Flew, Anthony, 143n.17
Fox, Christopher, 131n.4, 151n.32,
159–60n.17
Fraser, A. C., 12
*A Free but Modest Censure on the late
Controversial Writings . . . of the Lord
Bishop of Worcester and Mr. John
Locke*, 75, 89, 151n.25
French, Roger Kenneth, 160n.24
Frye, Northrop, 85, 153n.4

Garth, Sir Samuel: *The Dispensary*,
75, 76
Gay, John, 81. See also *Memoirs of . . .
Scriblerus*; Scriblerians
Gibson, James, 93
Gilson, Etienne, 15–16
Glanvill, Joseph, 92
Gray, James, 148n.4
Greene, Donald, 8
The Guardian, 48
Gulick, Charles B., 85
Gulliver's Travels (Swift), 78, 82, 87,
152n.33

Hagstrum, Jean H., 161n.35
Hale, Sir Matthew, 41

Harris, John, 38, 57–58, 59; *Lexicon
Technicum*, 38, 58
Hartle, Ann, 161n.31
Hearne, Thomas, 74
Heraclitus, 84, 123
The History of the Works of the Learned,
151n.25
Hobbes, Thomas, and bodily
identity, 140n.3
Holdsworth, Winch, 23, 38, 45, 70,
139n.38, 149n.8, 151n.25
Home, Henry, Lord Kames, 38,
143n.1
House of Lords, 41
Hughes, John, 149n.7
Human identity, as an equivocal
term, 30, 35, 58, 64
Hume, David: and consciousness,
59, 121; on issue of identity, 9–10,
70, 77; *My Own Life*, 132n.4; and
the passions, 125; on personal identity, 8, 9, 18, 19, 38, 59, 121; and
Pope, 125, 132n.4; and the Scriblerians, 105–6; and the soul, 122;
and spiritual substance, 93; *A
Treatise of Human Nature*, 2, 9, 57,
59, 69, 77, 121, 122, 125, 132n.4,
169

Identification with Christ, 77
Identity, 30. *See also* Human identity;
Personal identity; Principle of in-
dividuation; Puzzles of identity
Imagination, and memory, 63, 64;
and consciousness, 77–78
Immaterial substance. *See* Soul
Incarnation, 21, 43
Indivisibility of thought: and Clarke,
49; and Descartes, 17, 136–
37n.23; and Locke, 29, 141n.9;
and Scriblerians, 103
Insanity, 63, 77–78. *See also* Personal
identity; Puzzles of identity

Insubstantiality, 126–30. *See also*
Thinking, discontinuity of
Irenicum (Stillingfleet), 41

Johnson, Samuel, 59, 69, 90, 129,
147n.45, 148n.4; *Johnsonian
Miscellanies*, 69; *Preface to the
Dictionary*, 59; *Rasselas*, 69
Johnson, Samuel [the American],
127; *Elementa Philosophica: containing chiefly Noetica, or Things
relating to the Mind*, 160n.23

Kames, Lord. *See* Home, Henry
Lord Kames
Kant, Immanuel, 130
Keener, Frederick M., 150n.12
Kerby-Miller, Charles, 3, 81, 87,
157n.3. See also *Memoirs of . . .
Scriblerus*
Kersey, John, 99–100
King, William, 83, 89, 153n.10
Kirk, Eugene P., 153n.4
Kolb, Gwin J., 148n.4
Korkowski, Bud, 153n.4
Kristeller, Paul O., 88
Krutch, Joseph Wood, 18

Law, Edmund, 38, 129, 143n.1
LeClerc, Jean, 135n.13, 138n.32
Lee, Henry, 38, 101; *Anti-Scepticism:
Or, Notes upon each Chapter of Mr.
Lock's Essay Concerning Humane
Understanding*, 39–40, 43, 44, 47–
48, 60, 106, 127, 139n.30, 144–
45n.24, 158n.15; and conscious-
ness, 44, 48; and the substantial
self, 43, 45; and the soul, 44
Lee, Nathaniel (Nat), 63, 64, 77
Leibniz, Gottfried Wilhelm, 13, 64
*A Letter to Dr. Holdsworth, in Vindica-
tion of Mr. Locke* (Trotter), 70,
139n.38

*A Letter to the Right Reverend Edward
Ld Bishop of Worcester* (Locke),
42, 122
Levine, Joseph M., 58, 152n.3,
156n.29
Lexicon Technicum (Harris), 38, 57–58
Leyden, Wolfgang von, 17
Lloyd, A. C., 22
Lock, F. P., 153n.3
Locke, John: on Blackmore's poetry,
151n.26; and Browne, 122; and the
cogito, 29, 140n.6; and Collins, 48;
and concern, 33; on controversy,
155n.20; and Coste, 135n.13; and
Descartes, 28, 29, 49, 135–36n.14;
and free thinking, 151n.28 (see
also *Essay Concerning Human Understanding*); and French introspective
school, 72–73; and Garth, 75–76;
and Hobbes, 140n.3; and indivisibility of thought, 29, 141n.9; and
Molyneux, 65; and moral accountability, 56; and Perronet, 33,
62; and person, 32; and personal
identity, 2, 7, 18, 28, 60, 62, 63
(*see also* Locke's theory of personal
identity); and Pope, 20–21, 72–
73, 120–24; on puzzles of identity,
35–37, 60, 62, 78; and scholasticism, 92–93; and Scriblerians, 81–
117; and the self, 33, 62; and the
soul, 18, 29–31; and Swift, 19–20,
94; and theological concerns, 23,
139n.39; and thinking matter, 29,
43, 48, 106, 141n.11 (*see also*
Materialism)
—works: *Correspondence*, 27, 28, 38,
65, 69, 140nn. 2 and 3, 141n.7,
143n.7, 151n.26; *An Early Draft of
Locke's Essay*, 140n.6; *Educational
Writings*, 89; *Essay concerning Human
Understanding* (*see* individual entry); journals, 28; *A Letter to the*

Right Reverend Edward Ld Bishop of Worcester, 42, 122; *Mr. Locke's Reply to The Right Reverend the Lord Bishop of Worcester's Letter*, 93. *See also* Butler-Perronet debate; Clarke-Collins controversy; Locke-Stillingfleet controversy

The Locke Newsletter, 142n.14

Locke's theory of personal identity, 27–37; Berkeley on, 45–46, 62–63, 64; Butler on, 2, 10, 11, 14, 17–18, 45–46, 55–57, 59, 127; Clarke on (*see* Clarke-Collins controversy); Collins on (*see* Clarke-Collins controversy); and consciousness, 13–14, 18, 19, 32–33, 34–37, 38, 46, 73, 101, 106–7, 123, 134n.11, 135–36n.14; controversy over, 7–8, 9, 14, 37, 38–78 passim, 70; in *The Cyclopaedia*, 58–59; Felton on, 23, 70–71; and *Gulliver's Travels*, 78, 137–38n.29, 151–52n.33; Holdsworth on, 23, 70; implications of, 18, 47; inception of, 27–29, 140n.5; Nathaniel Lee on, 43–44, 47–48; and Leibniz, 64; in *Lexicon Technicum*, 57–58; and Molyneux, 27–28, 65; and Pope, 120–21; and Prior, 71–74; Thomas Reid on, 10, 47, 123; responses to, 17, 37, 38–68, 69–78, 138–39n.36, 142n.14; and the Resurrection, 37, 70; revolutionary nature of, 127; and Scriblerians, 20–21, 96–117; John Sergeant on, 44–45; and *The Spectator*, 1, 2, 36, 38, 59, 65–67; and Swift, 78; theological concerns in, 17, 21–24, 52, 139n.57; Catherine Trotter on, 37, 70; and Isaac Watts, 57, 63–65

Locke-Stillingfleet controversy, 23, 41–43, 71–76, 77–78, 92–93, 94, 151n.25, 152n.33, 155n.23, 159n.10

The London Journal (Boswell), 128

Lough, John, 146n.37

Lovejoy, A. O., 148n.2

Luce, A. A., 144n.17

Lucian, 83

Lucida Intervalla (Carkesse), 77–78

Ludus, 84–87. *See also* Menippean satire

Lund, Roger D., 153n.3

Lupton, Will, 139n.38

Lyons, J. O., 160–61n.31

Mack, Maynard, 138n.31

Maclean, Kenneth, 8–9, 20–21, 88, 117

McRae, Robert, 136n.14

Macrobius: *Saturnalia*, 83

Malebranche, Nicolas, 134–35n.13; *Recherche de la vérité*, 13

Malone, Edward, 109

Mandeville, Bernard, 38, 70

Materialism, 50, 101, 107; and the brain, 105; and Locke's theory of personal identity, 48, 106, 141n.11; and thinking matter, 43, 48, 105, 108, 141n.11, 144n.24

Maxwell, John, 69

Mayne, Charles. See *An Essay on Consciousness*

Mayne, Zachary. See *An Essay on Consciousness*

Meditations (Descartes), 17, 136–37n.23

Memoirs of the Extraordinary Life, Works, and Discoveries of Martinus Scriblerus, 78, 120; and Clarke-Collins controversy, 10, 48, 55, 101–9; and the deipnosophy, 83; and *Gulliver's Travels*, 87; personal identity defined, 2; publication of, 131; and puzzles of identity, 68,

Memoirs (continued)
110–17; and scholasticism, 92; and the substantial self, 129; quoted, 2, 81, 82, 83, 85, 87, 88–89, 90, 91, 96, 97, 98, 99, 100–116 passim; traditions of, 82–88. *See also* Arbuthnot, John; Gay, John; Oxford, Robert Harley; Parnell, Thomas; Pope, Alexander; Swift, Jonathan

Memoirs of what passed in Christendom from 1672 to 1679 (Temple), 31

Menippean satire, 83, 84, 86, 95, 153n.4

Miller, Perry, 8

A Miscellany of the Wits, 89

Misjuskovic, Ben Lazare, 141n.8

Molyneux, William, 27, 28, 64, 65; *Dioptrica Nova*, 27, 139–40n.2; and St. George Ashe, 139–40n.2

Montaigne, Michel de, 71–74; *The Essays of Michel Seigneur de Montaigne*, 71, 74

Moral accountability: and Butler, 56; Clarke on, 16, 52, 54–55, 108; and consciousness, 64; and Locke, 56; and personal identity, 14, 16, 28, 30, 36–37, 46–47, 52, 54–55, 57, 60, 108, 109, 110; and Siamese twins, 68; and the soul, 14–17; and temporary insanity, 64. *See also* Personal identity; Resurrection

Morris, John N., 128

Mossner, Ernest Campbell, 133n.4

Newton, Sir Isaac, 48

Nosce Teipsum (Davies), 15

"Of the Inconstancy of Our Actions" (Montaigne), 73

Oxford, Robert Harley, Earl of Oxford and Earl Mortimer, 81, 85. See also *Memoirs of . . . Scriblerus*; Scriblerians

Parfit, Derek, 142n.14

Parnell, Thomas, 81, 92, 155n.27. See also *Memoirs of . . . Scriblerus*; Scriblerians

Passions, the, and personal identity, 125

Patey, Douglas Lane, 158n.5

Pedantry, satire of, 82, 84–85, 87, 89

Perronet, Vincent, 62; *A Second Vindication of Mr. Locke, Wherein his Sentiments relating to Personal Identity are clear'd from some Mistakes of the Rev. Dr. Butler in his Dissertation on that Subject*, 33, 62, 70, 146n.31. *See also* Butler-Perronet debate; Perronet-Browne debate

Perronet-Browne debate, 142n.15

The Persian Tales, 66

Person: defined, 32, 58; early discussion of, 21–23; theological views on, 21

Personal identity: and Berkeley, 62–63; and Butler, 2; in Chambers's *Cyclopaedia*, 58–59; Clarke on, 16, 50–51; Collins on, 52–53; as controversial issue, 9, 10, 66, 69–72, 77; defined, 1, 2; Doddridge on, 119–20; and drunkenness, 65; and Hume, 8, 9, 18–19, 38, 59, 121; and insanity, 36, 37, 63, 77 (*see also* Puzzles of identity: Mad Man/Sober Man); and knowledge, 29, 42–43, 102–3, 121–23; and law, 48, 53, 55, 113–17, 158n.15; in *Lexicon Technicum*, 58; and Locke, 7, 10, 12, 28, 32–33, 60, 62, 93 (*see also* Locke's theory of personal identity); and moral accountability, 14, 16, 30, 46–47; and the passions, 125; as personal crisis, 128; Pope on, 120–25; in Prior, 71–72; problem of, 1, 114; Scriblerians on, 81–82, 120; and Martinus Scriblerus, 114; Shaftesbury

on, 1; and sleep, 65; in Stilling-
fleet, 43; in Swift, 77; as theologi-
cal concern, 14, 45, 138–39n.36;
and thinking about thinking, 73;
in Abraham Tucker, 119
Petronius: *Satyricon*, 83
Philosophical Essays on Various Subjects
(Watts), 28, 57, 63, 64–65, 71
Pirandello, Luigi, 18
Plato, 88
Plutarch: *Quaestiones*, 83
Pneumatology, 119
Poetry, and madness. *See* Carkesse,
James
Pope, Alexander, 38, 95, 127; and
Hume, 125, 132n.4; and Locke,
20–21, 72–73, 120–24, 138n.31;
and *The Memoirs*, 120; and Mon-
taigne, 72–74; and the passions,
125; and personal identity, 120–
25; and psychology, 120; and
scholasticism, 91; in Spence's
Anecdotes, 20, 72, 73, 83
—works: *The Art of Sinking in Poetry*,
82; *Correspondence*, 90; *The Dun-
ciad*, 82, 90, 91, 138n.32; *Epistle to
Cobham*, 120–26 passim; *An Essay
on Criticism*, 90; *An Essay on Man*,
121, 125; *Imitations of Horace*, 73,
86, 126. *See also Memoirs of . . .
Scriblerus*; Scriblerians
Popkin, Richard H., 144n.8
Porter, Noah, 133n.7
Poulet, Georges, 120–21
The Praise of Folly (Erasmus), 82
Preface to the Dictionary (Johnson), 59
Present State of the Republick of Letters,
154n.17
Prévost, Pierre, 12
Price, Martin, 82
Priestley, Joseph, 38, 143n.1
"Principium Individuationis." *See*
Hobbes, Thomas; Principle of
individuation

The Principles of Human Knowledge
(Berkeley), 19, 45, 93
Principle of individuation, 27, 58,
140n.3
Prior, Matthew, 38, 71–74; *A Dialogue Between Mr: John Lock and
Seigneur de Montaigne*, 69, 71–72;
and personal identity, 71–72
Probyn, Clive T., 152n.33, 156n.36
*Procedure, Extent and Limits of the
Human Understanding* (Browne),
122
Psychology, eighteenth-century, 3,
119, 120
Puzzles of identity, 34, 35, 59–68;
Briareus, 113–14; Drunken Man,
65; The Gallant Officer, 63,
147n.44; Mad Man/Sober Man,
36–37, 53, 55, 62, 64–65, 97,
147n.43; in *Memoirs of . . . Scriblerus*,
110–17; The Prince and the Cobbler, 36, 65–67; Siamese twins, 96,
109–16; the sleepwalker, 65; Socrates sleeping/Socrates waking,
37, 47–48, 78, 152n.34

Quintana, Ricardo, 137–38n.29

Rabb, Melinda Alliker, 126
Rasselas (Johnson), 69
Rational parrot, the, 31, 71–72,
141–42n.13
Rawson, C. J., 153n.3
Recherche de la vérité (Malebranche),
13
Reflection, 124
*Reflections on Mr. Clarke's Second
Defence. See* Collins, Anthony
*Reflections . . . touching the Doctrine of
the Trinity* (Tindal), 23
Regosin, Richard L., 74
Reid, Thomas, 9, 10, 38, 143n.1,
147n.44; *Essays on the Intellectual
Powers of Man*, 47, 123

Remarks upon An Essay Concerning Humane Understanding (Burnet), 39, 130

Remarks upon . . . the Rights of the Christian Church (Swift), 19–20, 23, 76, 93, 94

Reply to Mr. Clarke's Defence. See Collins, Anthony

Resurrection, 21, 23, 61, 68; Boyle on, 22; Clarke on, 52, 54–55, 108; and consciousness, 37, 43, 70; and Locke's theory of personal identity, 23, 37; and Stillingfleet, 43. *See also* Moral accountability; Personal identity

Resurrection of the same Numerical Body . . . In which Mr. Lock's Notions of Personality and Identity are confuted (Felton), 70

Richardson, Samuel, 9, 127

Rooy, C. A. Van, 153n.7

Rorty, Amélie Oskenberg, 14, 142n.14

Rosa and Josepha, 109

Royal Society of London, 57, 58

St. James Palace, 19

Satura, 84, 86. *See also* Menippean satire

Saturnalia (Macrobius), 83

A Satyr Against Wit (Blackmore), 76

Sayce, R. A., 73–74

Scholasticism, 91–95, 100–101, 155n.27

Scriblerians, 14, 85, 86; on Clarke-Collins debate, 101–9; and consciousness, 103–9; on controversy, 89–90; and Hume, 105–6; and intellectual issues, 87–88; on the legal profession, 113–16; on Locke's theory of personal identity, 20–21, 96–117; on logic and metaphysics, 88–92, 97–101; and Men-

ippean satire, 95; and personal identity, 81–82, 120; and philosophical issues, 19; and scholasticism, 91, 92, 93–95, 100–101; and Siamese twins, 117; and the substantial self, 97–101. *See also* Arbuthnot, John; Gay, John; *Memoirs of . . . Scriblerus*; Parnell, Thomas; Pope, Alexander; Swift, Jonathan

Scriblerian satire, aims of, 81–82. *See also* Scriblerians

Scriblerus, Martinus. See *Memoirs of . . . Scriblerus*

Scriblerus Club. *See* Scriblerians

A Second Vindication of Mr. Locke. See Perronet, Vincent

Selby, Hopewell, 152n.3

Self, defined: in Locke, 33; in Collins, 52–53; in Montaigne, 73–74. *See also* Personal identity

Senility, 37, 60–61

Sentiment, and consciousness, 12, 136n.14

Sergeant, John, 38, 44–45, 46, 48; *Solid Philosophy Asserted, Against the Fancies of the Ideists*, 45, 47, 107

A Sermon . . . in which the Cavils . . . of Mr. Locke and others, against the Resurrection of the Same Body, are examin'd. See Holdsworth, Winch

Sex and logic, in *Memoirs of . . . Scriblerus*, 86

Shaftesbury, Anthony, Earl of, 41

Shaftesbury, Anthony Ashley Cooper, 3d Earl of, 1, 2, 7, 38, 91, 147n.43, 159n.12

Sherlock, William: *A Defence of Dr. Sherlock's Notion of a Trinity in Unity*, 23

Shoemaker, Sydney, 142n.14

Siamese twins, 67–68, 96–97, 109–16. *See also* Rosa and Josepha

Sitter, John, 120

Smith, John, 15
Solid Philosophy Asserted, Against the Fancies of the Ideists (Sergeant), 45, 47, 107
Solipsism, 72
Some Physico-Theological Considerations about the Possibility of the Resurrection (Boyle), 22
Soul: and animal spirits, 144–45n.25; as candle, 130; and Clarke-Collins controversy, 48–49, 51, 52; commentary on, 15, 18, 22, 29–31, 44, 122; and empiricism (*see* Thinking, discontinuity of); and epistemic turn, 29–30, 41–43, 93, 101–3, 121–22, 129–30; indivisibility of, 15, 17, 29, 49, 103–4, 130, 141n.9; and moral accountability, 14–17; and personal identity, 31, 60–61; pre-existence of, 35; seat of, 101–2, 114; in Siamese twins, 68; transfer of, 65–66; transmigration of, 31, 35. *See also* Substantial self
Spacks, Patricia Meyer, 9, 161n.31
The Spectator, 1, 36, 38, 59, 65–67, 69
Spence, Joseph, 20, 73, 135n.13, 138n.31
Stearne, Dean, 68
Steele, Sir Richard. See *The Spectator*
Steensma, Robert C., 152–53n.3
Sterne, Laurence: *Tristram Shandy*, 1, 82, 119, 127
Stewart, Dugald, 12, 19, 95, 97
Stewart, M. A., 22
Stillingfleet, Edward, 23, 38, 40, 41–43, 48, 52, 71, 76, 101, 102, 121–22; and *Gulliver's Travels*, 78, 137–38n.29, 151–52n.33
—works: *The Bishop of Worcester's Answer to Mr. Locke's Second Letter, Wherein his Notion of Ideas Is prov'd to be Inconsistent with it self And with the Articles of the Christian Faith*, 40,

43, 59, 102, 121; *A Discourse in Vindication of the Doctrine of the Trinity*, 9, 23, 41–42, 76, 159n.12; *Irenicum*, 41. *See also* Berkeley, George; Locke-Stillingfleet controversy; Stillingfleetians; Swift, Jonathan
Stillingfleetians, 45, 74–77, 151n.25
Subconscious, the, 130
Substance, 31, 41, 42, 45, 92, 93, 98, 102, 105, 141n.10
Substantia cogitans, 17
Substantial self, the: Berkeley on, 45–46, 98; Robert Boyle on, 22; Thomas Burnet on, 130; Butler on, 11, 14, 56; Clarke on, 52; critique of, 29, 30–31, 34–35, 99; Ralph Cudworth on, 15; Sir John Davies on, 15; defense of, 40 46, 50, 60, 61–62, 70; Descartes on, 16, 17; and empiricism, 42, 102–3, 121, 124–25, 127–30; Etienne Gilson on, 15–16; and Hume, 122; and later movements in thought, 161n.30; and Nathaniel Lee, 43, 45; and Locke, 8, 18, 22, 29–31, 34–35, 93, 98, 102; Montaigne on, 74; Pope on, 122–23; and problem of finding, 129; Scriblerians on, 98–109, 113–15; and John Smith on, 15. *See also* Soul
Swift, Jonathan, 27, 31, 76, 78; on Aristotle, 94; on controversy, 89; and Locke, 19–20, 78, 94; and personal identity, 77; and the rational parrot, 31; and scholasticism, 91–92, 94, 155n.27; and Siamese twins, 67–68
—works: *Correspondence*, 67–68; "The Dean's Reasons For not Building at Drapier's Hill," 92; *Gulliver's Travels*, 78, 82, 87, 152n.33; "On the Trinity," 89–90, 94; *Remarks upon . . . the Rights of the Christian*

Swift, works (continued)
  Church, 19–20, 23, 76, 93, 94; *A
  Tale of a Tub,* 77–78, 82, 92. See
  also *The Memoirs of . . . Scriblerus*
Swinburne, Richard, 142n.14
Syme, Sir Ronald, 136n.15

A Tale of a Tub (Swift), 77–78, 82,
  92
The Task (Cowper), 129
Temple, Sir William, 89, 141n.13;
  *Memoirs of what passed in Christendom
  from 1672 to 1679,* 31
Tennant, R. C., 142–43n.16
Thiel, Udo, 142nn. 14 and 16
Thinking, discontinuity of, 29, 49–
  50, 53, 54, 101, 103, 121–23, 130
Thinking about thinking, 72–73,
  150n.15
Thinking matter. *See* Locke, John;
  Materialism
Third Defence. See Clarke, Samuel
*Three Dialogues Between Hylas and
  Philonous* (Berkeley), 45, 46, 123
Tillotson, John, 41
Tindal, Matthew, 19, 20, 23, 76; and
  Locke, 94; *Reflexions . . . touching the
  Doctrine of the Trinity,* 23; *Rights of
  the Christian Church,* 94. *See also*
  Swift, Jonathan
Toland, John, 20, 41
*Tractatus . . . de Persona. Or, A Trea-
  tise of the Word Person* (Clendon),
  15
Traugott, John, 156n.36
Treatise against Eutyches and Nestorius
  (*Boethius*), 15, 21
A Treatise of Human Nature. See
  Hume, David
*A Treatise of the Hypochondriack and
  Hysteric Passions* (Mandeville),
  70
Trinitarian controversy, 139n.37

Trinity, 43
Tristram Shandy (Sterne), 1, 82, 119,
  127
Trotter, Catherine (Catherine Trot-
  ter Cockburn), 37, 38, 149n.8;
  *A Defence of The Essay of Human
  Understanding,* 37; *A Letter to Dr.
  Holdsworth, in Vindication of Mr.
  Locke,* 70, 139n.38
Tucker, Abraham, 38, 119, 143n.1
Tuveson, Ernest Lee, 18, 20, 132n.1
*Two Dissertations Concerning Sense
  and the Imagination. With an Essay
  on Consciousness. See An Essay on
  Consciousness*

Varro, 83, 84
Viner, Jacob, 143n.6

Walker, Robert G., 148n.4
Warburton, the Reverend William,
  21
Warton, Thomas, 157n.3
Watt, Ian, 7, 127
Watts, Isaac, 38, 45, 57, 62, 63–65,
  77, 138–39n.36, 139n.38, 149n.10,
  152n.34; *Philosophical Essays on
  Various Subjects,* 28, 57, 63, 64–65,
  71
Webb, C. J. Clement, 161n.38
Wesley, Charles, 142n.15
Whytt, Robert, 69, 127
Willey, Basil, 8, 132n.2
Williams, Aubrey L., 155n.24
Woodruff, James F., 153n.3
Woodward, John, 82; *Essay Toward
  a Natural History of the Earth,* 58
Wotton, William, 154n.17

Yolton, John, 3, 8, 9, 23, 135n.13,
  139nn. 37 and 39, 140n.5, 141n.11,
  150n.15
Young, Edward, 129

Compositor: Asco Trade Typesetting Ltd.
       Text: 12/14 Baskerville
    Display: Helvetica Condensed and Baskerville
    Printer: Braun-Brumfield, Inc.
     Binder: Braun-Brumfield, Inc.